CW00456002

Welcome

CONDÉ NAST JOHANSENS

30

1982–2012

ANNIVERSARY

Welcome to the 30th anniversary edition of Recommended Small Hotels, Inns & Restaurants, Great Britain & Ireland.

For three decades we have visited and inspected hotels throughout Great Britain and Ireland. Some hotels have been recommended almost continuously from the first 'Derek Johansens' Guide published in 1982. Their continued inclusion can be attributed to their enduring and absolute belief in placing the needs of their guests first. So look out for the 30th Anniversary roundel at the top of their page entry!

We know from your letters and e-mails that you expect the highest standards of accommodation and service and we have set out to match those expectations by our Recommendations within this Guide for 2012.

You can share your experiences by giving Condé Nast Johansens Gift Vouchers to your friends and family. The vouchers can be redeemed at any of our 2012 Recommendations and make a much valued gift for anniversaries and other special occasions. Purchase them at www.condenastjohansens.com/gift-vouchers.

We are always pleased to receive your comments and feedback. The quickest and easiest way to pass on your views is via "Tell us about your stay" at the foot of each hotel page entry on: www.condenastjohansens.com. Finally, don't forget to mention that you are a Condé Nast Johansens Guide user when making an enquiry or a booking. You should receive a very warm welcome when you arrive.

Andrew Warren
Managing Director

The Windermere Suites, Cumbria, England – p33

1

LIQUID ASSETS

About this Guide

To find a hotel by location:

- Use the **county maps** at the front of the Guide to obtain a page number for the area of the country you wish to search.

- Turn to the **indexes** at the back of the Guide, which start on page 148.

- Alternatively, use the maps at the front of each colour coded country section where each hotel is marked.

If you cannot find a suitable hotel you may decide to choose one of the properties within the Condé Nast Johansens Recommended Hotels & Spas Guide. These establishments are listed on pages 113–120.

Once you have made your choice please contact the hotel directly. Rates are per room, including VAT and breakfast (unless stated otherwise) and are correct at the time of going to press but you should always check with the hotel before you make your reservation. When making a booking please mention Condé Nast Johansens as your source of reference.

Readers should be aware that by making a reservation with a hotel, either by telephone, e-mail or in writing, they are entering into a legal contract. A hotelier under certain circumstances is entitled to make a charge for accommodation when guests fail to arrive, even if notice of the cancellation is given.

Inveran Lodge, Highland, Scotland – p97

Recommendations can be found plotted on more detailed maps at the front of each colour coded country section

Higland p95

Argyll & Bute
p90

SCOTLAND

Dumfries & Galloway p92

N. IRELAND

Monaghan p87

Dublin p86

IRELAND

ENGLAND

WALES

SCOTLAND

N. IRELAND

IRELAND

WALES

ENGLAND

Northumberland p58

Cumbria p31

North Yorkshire p81

Lancashire p56

West Yorkshire p83

Conwy p103

Gwynedd p104

Derbyshire p36

Nottinghamshire p59

Staffordshire p71

Shropshire p65

Ceredigion p102

Worcestershire p79

Norfolk p57

Herefordshire p50

Suffolk p72

Bedfordshire p26

Monmouthshire p108

Gloucestershire p44

Oxfordshire p61

Essex p43

Somerset p67

Wiltshire p78

Surrey p76

Hampshire p48

Kent p54

Devon p37

Dorset p42

Cornwall p28

Isle of Wight p52

Channel Islands

Guernsey p14

Jersey p15

5

Key to Symbols

🛏 23   Total number of bedrooms

🌿   The property participates in a minimum of 3 environmentally-friendly practices specified by Condé Nast Johansens

🏠   The property is owner managed

⚲   The property is available for exclusive use

🦢   The property is situated in a quiet location

♿   Wheelchair access – we recommend contacting the property to determine the level of accessibility for wheelchair users

👨‍🍳   The property has a chef-patron (the owner of the property is also the chef at the restaurant)

Ⓜ 23   Maximum capacity for meeting/conference facilities on-site

👪 8   Children are welcome, with minimum age where applicable

🐕   Dogs are welcome in bedrooms or kennels

🛏   At least 1 bedroom has a four-poster bed

📺   Cable/satellite TV in all bedrooms

🔊   Some or all bedrooms provide an iPod docking station

📞   ISDN/modem point available in all bedrooms

WiFi   Wireless internet connection available in all rooms

🚬   Smoking is allowed in some bedrooms

🛗   A lift available for guests' use

❄   Air conditioning is available in all bedrooms

🏋   Gym/fitness facilities are available on-site

SPA   The property has a dedicated spa with on-site qualified staff and an indoor pool, offering extensive body, beauty and water treatments

🌊   Indoor swimming pool on-site

🌊   Outdoor swimming pool on-site

🎾   Tennis court on-site

🚶   Walking – details of local walking routes, an overnight drying room for clothes and packed lunches can be provided by the property

🎣   Fishing on-site

🎣   Fishing can be arranged nearby

⛳   Golf course on-site

🏌   Golf course is available nearby

🎯   Shooting on-site

🔫   Shooting can be arranged nearby

🐎   Horse riding on-site

🐴   Horse riding can be arranged nearby

🚁   The property has a helicopter landing pad

🔔   The property is licensed for wedding ceremonies

Centre of Attention

Freestanding baths are back. With modern, eye-catching designs, the new KOHLER® Lithocast™ baths make a bold design statement sure to be the focal point of any bathing space.

Discover KOHLER®
A world of innovative and inspiring bathroom design awaits.

+44 (0) 844 571 0048
kohler.co.uk

THE BOLD LOOK
OF **KOHLER**®

Old Swan & Minster Mill, Oxfordshire, England – p63

Condé Nast Johansens

Condé Nast Johansens Ltd, 6-8 Old Bond Street, London W1S 4PH
Tel: +44 (0)20 7499 9080 Fax: +44 (0)20 7152 3565
E-mail: info@johansens.com www.condenastjohansens.com

Hotel Inspectors:	Tim Fay
	John Morison
	Mary O'Neill
	Andrew Warren
Marketing Manager:	Adam Crabtree
Digital Marketing Manager:	Gemma James
Production Manager:	Kevin Bradbrook
Production Editor:	Laura Kerry
Senior Designer:	Rory Little
Copywriters:	Stephanie Cook
	Sasha Creed
	Norman Flack
	Debra O'Sullivan
	Rozanne Paragon
Client Services Director:	Fiona Patrick
PA to Managing Director:	Amelia Priday
Managing Director:	Andrew Warren

Whilst every care has been taken in the compilation of this Guide, the publishers cannot accept responsibility for any inaccuracies or for changes since going to press, or for consequential loss arising from such changes or other inaccuracies, or for any other loss direct or consequential arising in connection with information describing establishments in this publication.

Recommended establishments, if accepted for inclusion, pay an annual subscription to cover the costs of inspection, the distribution and production of copies placed in hotel bedrooms and other services.

Condé Nast Johansens Ltd. is part of The Condé Nast Publications Ltd.
ISBN 978-1-903665-58-9
Printed in Scotland by Scotprint, Haddington.
Distributed in the UK and Europe by Portfolio, Brentford (bookstores). In North America by Casemate Publishing, Pennsylvania (bookstores).

L'Instant Champagne, with *Vitalie Taittinger*.

Vitalie Taittinger is an active member of the family Champagne House.

CHAMPAGNE **TAITTINGER**
Reims
Champagne for the Independently Minded

Pen-Y-Dyffryn Country Hotel, Shropshire, England – p65

Awards for Excellence

The Condé Nast Johansens 2011 Awards for Excellence were presented at the Condé Nast Johansens Annual Dinner held at The May Fair hotel, London on 8th November 2010. Awards were given to properties from all over the world that represent the finest standards and best value for money in luxury independent travel. An important source of information for these awards was the feedback provided by guests who completed Condé Nast Johansens Guest Survey Reports.

Please nominate a hotel via its entry page on www.condenastjohansens.com, under "Tell us about your stay."

2011 Winners appearing in this Guide:

Most Excellent Inn
• The Cary Arms – Devon, England, p37

Most Excellent Value for money
• Pen-Y-Dyffryn Country Hotel– Shropshire, England, p65

Most Excellent Innovation in Sustainable Hospitality
• The Traddock – North Yorkshire, England, p81

Channel Islands

GUERNSEY

La Fontenelle

St Sampson

Saint Peter Port

Richmond

La Planque

HERM ISLAND

St Anne

ALDERNEY

SARK

14

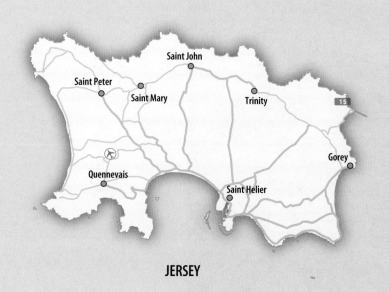

Saint John

Saint Peter

Saint Mary

Trinity

15

Quennevais

Gorey

Saint Helier

JERSEY

La Sablonnerie, Guernsey, Channel Islands – p14

For further information on the Channel Islands, please contact:

Visit Guernsey
Tel: +44 (0)1481 723552
E-mail: enquiries@visitguernsey.com
www.visitguernsey.com

Jersey Tourism
Tel: +44 (0)1534 448800
E-mail: info@jersey.com
www.jersey.com

Sark Tourism
Tel: +44 (0)1481 832345
E-mail: contact@sark.info
www.sark.info

Aurigny Air Services
E-mail: res@aurigny.com
www.aurigny.com

or see **pages 122-124** for details of local historic houses, castles and gardens to visit during your stay.

For additional places to stay in the Channel Islands, turn to **pages 113-120** where a listing of our Recommended Hotels & Spas Guide can be found.

LA SABLONNERIE

LITTLE SARK, SARK, GUERNSEY GY9 0SD
Tel: 01481 832061 **International:** +44 (0)1481 832061
Web: www.condenastjohansens.com/lasablonnerie **E-mail:** lasablonnerie@cwgsy.net

Our inspector loved: Riding in a horse drawn carriage and arriving at this delightful little haven of good food, wine and good company!

Price Guide: (including dinner)
single from £78
double/twin £156–£290

Awards/Recognition: 2 AA Rosette 2011-2012

Location: Via St Peter Port, Guernsey, 45-min ferry

Attractions: George's boat trip around the island; Cycling, walking, swimming and bird watching; Champagne and lobsters; La Seigneurie Gardens

Owner and manager Elizabeth Perrée considers La Sablonnerie an oasis of good living and courtesy rather than a luxurious hotel. It is an hotel of rare quality situated in a time warp of simplicity on a tiny, idyllic island where no motor cars are allowed and life ambles along at a peaceful unhurried pace. A vintage horse drawn carriage collects guests from Sark's tiny harbour. Tranquil cosiness, friendliness and sophistication characterise this hotel with its low ceilings and 400-year-old oak beams. Elizabeth has extended and discreetly modernised the hotel with bedrooms which are charmingly individual in style. The hotel has a reputation for superb cuisine. Many of the dishes are prepared from produce grown on its own farm and in its gardens, and enhanced by locally caught lobster and oysters.

CHÂTEAU LA CHAIRE

ROZEL BAY, JERSEY JE3 6AJ
Tel: 01534 863354 **International:** +44 (0)1534 863354
Web: www.condenastjohansens.com/chateaulachaire **E-mail:** res@chateau-la-chaire.co.uk

Our inspector loved: *This hidden gem with traditional charms and romantic overtones!*

Price Guide: (inclusive of morning paper and afternoon tea)
classic double from £120
superior double from £170
suite from £220

Awards/Recognition: 2 AA Rosettes 2011-2012

Location: A6, 1.5 miles; St Helier, 7 miles; Jersey Airport, 11 miles

Attractions: The Durrell Wildlife Conservation Trust; Jersey Pottery; Occupation Museum; Stunning Coastal Scenery

You can see that care and great attention to detail are important at this charming hotel located just a short walk from Rozel Bay. Built in 1843 as a rather grand elegant home, today's owners have kept many original antiques and classical paintings to enhance the period charm to this romantic place. Nestled high in a wooded valley close to the sea, this is a great location from which to explore the island. The garden, currently awaiting restoration, will delight botanists. An excellent reputation follows the oak-panelled restaurant with a menu full of both Gallic and English influences whilst the sunny terrace seems a popular place for locals to catch up on news and chat during the islands many warm months.

North West England

Berwick-Upon-Tweed

SCOTLAND

Northumberland
National Park

Carlisle

Lake District
National Park

Windermere

| 31 | 33 |
| 32 | 35 |
| 34 |

Kendal

Yorkshire Dales
National Park

Isle
of
Man

Douglas

Barrow-in-
Furness

Fleetwood

Skipton

81

Blackpool

Preston

56

Southport

Bolton

Wigan

Manchester

Liverpool

Liverpool

Manchester

WALES

North East England

Berwick-Upon-Tweed

Alnwick

Newcastle

Durham

Middlesbrough

Teeside

North York Moors
National Park

Thirsk

Skipton

Harrogate

York

Hull

Leeds
Bradford

Halifax

Wakefield

Huddersfield

Doncaster

Sheffield

Lincoln

Central England

Peak District National park

Manchest... Manchester Liverpool Chester Whitchurch Shrewsbury Stoke Buxton Sheffield Doncaster Chesterfield Derby Nottingham Grantham Leicester Kettering Northampton Milton Keynes Wolverhampton Bridgnorth Birmingham Kidderminster Ludlow Stratford-upon-Avon Worcester Hereford Ross-on-Wye Cheltenham Gloucester Cirencester Oxford

East Midlands Birmingham

WALES

Eastern England

Louth

Lincoln

Cromer

A148

The Broads

King's Lynn

Norwich

Great Yarmouth

Peterborough

Thetford

A1066

Newmarket

Bury St Edmunds

Cambridge

Ipswich

Felixstowe

Bishop's Stortford

Stansted

Colchester

Luton

Chelmsford

19

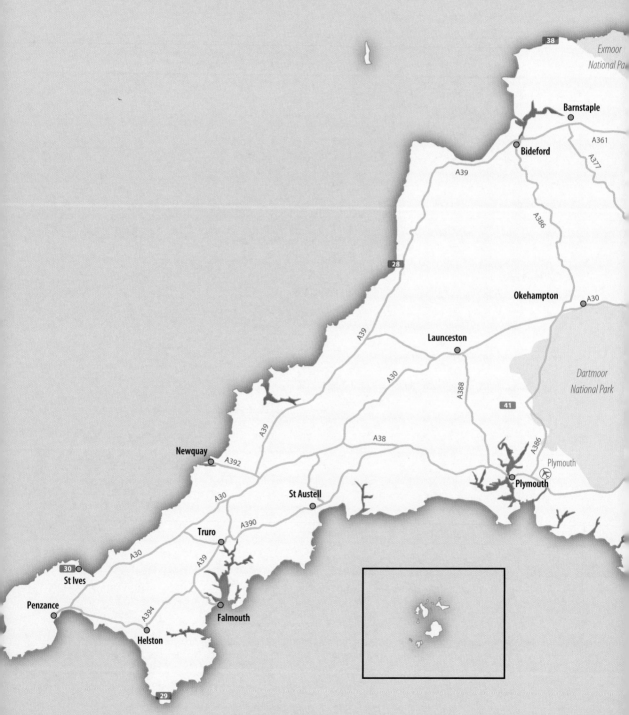

South West England

WALES

Exmoor
National Pa...

38

Barnstaple

Bideford

A361

A377

A39

A386

28

Okehampton

A30

Launceston

A39

A30

A388

Dartmoor
National Park

41

Newquay

A38

A392

A39

A386

Plymouth

A30

Plymouth

St Austell

Truro

A390

A39

A30

30

St Ives

A394

Penzance

Helston

29

WALES

South West England

Bristol ✈

Bristol

Bath

A48

M5

A429

M4

A46

78

A4174

A4174

A4

A38

67

A37

A350

A361

A39

Warminster

70 69

A36

M5

A37

A303

Taunton

A358

A303

42

A350

A354

A361

M5

A37

Yeovil

Blandford Forum

A377

Exeter ✈

A30

A35

Bridport

A35

Bournen

Bournem

A30

A38

Exeter

Dorchester

A354

Weymouth

39

Exmoor
National Park

68

A380

40

Torquay

37

A385

Kingsbridge

Southern England

Milton Keynes

Brackley

Stow-on-the-Wold

Cheltenham

Aylesbury

Oxford

Luto

Cirencester

Swindon

Marlborough

Reading

Windsor

Heathrow

Newbury

Basingstoke

Guildford

Winchester

Salisbury

Southampton

Southampton

New Forest

Chichester

Bournemouth

Portsmouth

Bognor Regis

Bournemouth

Cowes

Isle
of
Wight

South East England

Felixstowe

Stansted

Colchester

Hertford

Chelmsford

Sheerness

Ramsgate

GREATER
LONDON

City

Dartford

Canterbury

Maidstone

Gatwick

Tonbridge

Ashford

Dover

East
Grinstead

Royal
Tunbridge
Wells

Folkestone

Uckfield

Brighton

Hastings

Newhaven

Eastbourne

Gold Key Media

Gold Key Media is the World's largest supplier of magazines to the hotel and leisure industry. We have a range of over 200 international magazine titles to chose from at the most competitive prices available. We help you to ensure your guests relax in the comfort of your hotel and spa.

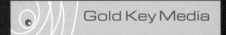

Gold Key Media is proud to supply the most desirable and recognised hotels and venues in the world.
We work with the most established and recognised titles in the publishing industry to provide you with the best discounts on Newspaper and Magazine volumes for your business.
All our clients are given a dedicated and personalised service.
www.goldkeymedia.co.uk or call +44 (0) 20 7491 4065

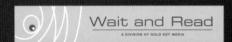

Wait and read provide quality magazine subscription packs for businesses at exceptional discounts.
Save up to 80% off the cover price.
No Minimum Orders.
Courier Deliveries
Direct Debit Option.
Create your bespoke pack from over 100 monthly and weekly titles.
www.waitandread.co.uk or call +44 (0) 18 9543 3733

MAGAZINE CAFÉ

Offering single issue, single copy to full-year subscriptions of your favourite magazines, you need never miss an issue again.
Magazine Café offers UK and international magazines in all categories to suit all tastes, whether for yourself or as a gift. Whatever you are interested in reading about, Magazine Café has it covered.
To see the extensive selection of international titles and details of how to order, please go to our website.
www.magazinecafe.co.uk or call +44 (0) 18 9543 3722

The Pig Hotel, Hampshire, England – p48

England

For further information on England, please contact:

Cumbria Tourist Board
www.cumbriatourism.org

East of England Tourist Board
Tel: +44 (0)1284 727470
E-mail: info@eet.org.uk
www.visiteastofengland.com

Heart of England Tourism
www.visittheheart.co.uk

Visit London
Tel: 0870 156 6366
www.visitlondon.com

North East England Tourism Team
www.visitnortheastengland.com

North West Tourist Board
www.visitenglandsnorthwest.com

Tourism South East
Tel: +44 (0)23 8062 5400
www.visistsoutheastengland.com

South West Tourism
Tel: 0870 442 0880
E-mail: info@swtourism.org.uk
www.swtourism.co.uk

Welcome to Yorkshire
E-mail: info@yorkshire.com
www.yorkshire.com

English Heritage
Tel: +44 (0)870 333 1181
www.english-heritage.org.uk

Historic Houses Association
Tel: +44 (0)20 7259 5688
E-mail: info@hha.org.uk
www.hha.org.uk

The National Trust
Tel: 0844 800 1895
www.nationaltrust.org.uk

or see **pages 122-124** for details of local historic houses, castles and gardens to visit during your stay.

For additional places to stay in England, turn to **pages 113-120** where a listing of our Recommended Hotels & Spas Guide can be found.

CORNFIELDS RESTAURANT & HOTEL

WILDEN ROAD, COLMWORTH, BEDFORDSHIRE MK44 2NJ
Tel: 01234 378990 **International:** +44 (0)1234 378990
Web: www.condenastjohansens.com/cornfields **E-mail:** reservations@cornfieldsrestaurant.co.uk

Our inspector loved: *The great food and lovely rural setting.*

Price Guide:
single £90
double £150
four poster £165

Location: A1, 3 miles; M1, 9 miles, A421, 3 miles Bedford, 5 miles Cambridge, 30 mins; London Luton Airport, 40 mins

Attractions: Cambridge; Cecil Higgins Gallery in Bedford; Woburn; Grafham Water

Nestling in the undulating Bedfordshire countryside Cornfields Restaurant & Hotel is a haven for those in search of a peaceful retreat to unwind and indulge. The inn dates back to the 17th century and features original beams and an inglenook fireplace. King-size beds invite guests to retire in the spacious, individually appointed bedrooms. However, the property's true appeal lies in its cuisine and its owners' vision to create freshly cooked dishes using locally sourced produce. Starters such as stilton, walnut and bacon fritters with a redcurrant and port sauce are delicious and main courses available include British classics such as pork with mild grain mustard and caramelised apples. The smaller of the 2 dining rooms can be hired for private use and is ideal for exclusive dining or business meetings.

FLITWICK MANOR

CHURCH ROAD, FLITWICK, BEDFORDSHIRE MK45 1AE
Tel: 01525 712242 **International:** +44 (0)1525 712242
Web: www.condenastjohansens.com/flitwickmanor **E-mail:** flitwick@menzieshotels.co.uk

Our inspector loved: *The beautiful grounds and centuries of history that make this a fascinating place to stay.*

Price Guide:
single £110
double/twin £150
executive £190

Awards/Recognition: 1 AA Rosette 2011-2012

Location: A5120; M1 jct 12 North, 4 miles; M1 jct 13 South, 8 miles; London, 40-min train; London Luton Airport, 15 miles

Attractions: Ascott House; Waddesdon Manor Stately Home; Woburn Abbey and Safari Park; Woburn Golf Course

For an enticing escape to a country estate, look no further than this classic Georgian hotel, Flitwick Manor. Food lovers in particular will appreciate the restaurant, where they can enjoy the very best in British and European food, before retiring to an elegantly furnished room or suite complete with four poster bed. The hotel is enhanced with antiques and period pieces, and outside, the pretty gardens reveal a tennis court and croquet lawn. If you're travelling on business Flitwick offers 3 charming function suites, and a Premier Meetings package means you can plan every last detail with a dedicated team. Weddings and other celebrations are also very much catered for, and guests can experience a full taste of country living when hiring the house for exclusive use. This is simply the perfect place to unwind, with much to discover in nearby Woburn with its listed buildings, boutiques and Safari Park.

Elements Hotel and Restaurant

MARINE DRIVE, WIDEMOUTH BAY, BUDE, CORNWALL EX23 0LZ
Tel: 01288 352386 **International:** +44 (0)1288 352386
Web: www.condenastjohansens.com/elements **E-mail:** surf@elements-life.co.uk

Our inspector loved: The relaxed atmosphere, excellent bistro with spectacular sea views and the wide choice of outdoor activities on offer nearby.

Price Guide:
single £47.50-£52.50
double £95-£105
family £125-£135

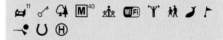

Location: A39; Bude, 2 miles; Newquay Airport, 37.5 miles; Exeter, 63.5 miles

Attractions: Tintagel; Padstow; Port Isaac; Eden Project

Set high on the cliffs between Bude and Widemouth Bay with breathtaking panoramic views, this delightful boutique-style hotel and Italian restaurant is one of the finest and trendiest new editions to this beautiful part of North Cornwall. With a newly refurbished bar and restaurant area that features a terrace, elements is rightly gaining a reputation as one of the coolest venues in the region offering exceptional Italian cuisine. Everything in the recently renovated bedrooms, such as the sumptuous Relyon beds, makes for a welcoming and relaxing stay. And amenities include a state-of-the-art 4 station multi gym and classic Finholme sauna for those seeking respite after an activity filled day, by or in the water. Don't miss out on the excellent surfing lessons run by former European champion Mike Raven here at Widemouth Bay and make use of the hotel's complimentary foam surfboards and mountain bikes to fully enjoy your surroundings.

ATLANTIC HOUSE

PENTREATH LANE, LIZARD, CORNWALL TR12 7NY
Tel: 01326 290399 **International:** +44 (0)1326 290399
Web: www.condenastjohansens.com/atlantichselizard **E-mail:** atlantichse@aol.com

Our inspector loved: The warm welcome and great location on the famous Lizard.

Price Guide:
double/twin £100-£150

Location: B3083, 220 yards; Helston, 10 miles; Newquay Airport, 46.5 miles;

Attractions: Kynance Cove; Trevarno Gardens; St Michael's Mount; St Ives

Located down a quiet lane, yet close to the dramatic Cornish coast, the setting of this Edwardian house is picture perfect and the fact it is The Lizard Peninsula's only 5-star luxury B&B and a recipient of Visit England's Gold Award makes it an irresistible place to escape the pace of modern life. Whether it's a romantic break, walking holiday or weekend getaway you're after, you'll find that this bright, sunny guest house, complete with charming hosts, ticks all the boxes. Bedrooms feature heavenly beds, feather pillows and organic handmade toiletries, and most rooms have views too large to capture on camera. The South West Coast Path is just 10 minutes away, and after a long day's walking relax in a comfy leather sofa and watch the ships sail by, or soak in the tub. Feel free to bring your own wine; glasses and corkscrews are provided. There is no restaurant here but there are many excellent options nearby, and the delicious breakfasts will more than set you up for the day.

29

THE GARRACK HOTEL & RESTAURANT

BURTHALLAN LANE, ST IVES, CORNWALL TR26 3AA
Tel: 01736 796199 **International:** +44 (0)1736 796199
Web: www.condenastjohansens.com/garrack **E-mail:** djenquiry@garrack.com

Our inspector loved: The hill top location with its coastal views of St Ives and the great food.

Price Guide:
single £75–£110
double/twin £134–£220

Awards/Recognition: 1 AA Rosette 2011-2012

Location: B3306, 0.65 mile; A3074, 1 mile; A30, 5 miles; Newquay Airport, 27 miles

Attractions: Porthmeor Beach; St Ives Tate Gallery; The Leach Pottery; Coastal Paths

This Kilby family run hotel is set in 2 picturesque acres of gardens with fabulous sea views and nearby coastal walks. Wander down the hill to Porthmeor beach and its excellent surf, St Ives' old town or the St Ives Tate Gallery, then back up, for a steep, but scenic walk. Bedrooms in the original house maintain the style of the building, while additional rooms are modern in design. A ground floor room has been equipped for guests with disabilities. Lounges have open fires, and a bijou leisure centre contains a small pool, sauna and fitness area. Service is informal yet professional, and the restaurant specialises in seafood, especially fresh lobster. With 70 selected wines. Gateway to wonderful coastal walks, dogs are welcome by prior arrangement.

APPLEGARTH VILLA

COLLEGE ROAD, WINDERMERE, CUMBRIA LA23 1BU
Tel: 015394 43206 **International:** +44 (0)15394 43206
Web: www.condenastjohansens.com/applegarth **E-mail:** info@lakesapplegarth.co.uk

Our inspector loved: *Sitting on the secluded terrace watching the sun set over the Langdale Pikes.*

Price Guide:
single £62-£120
double £130-£210

Location: Windermere Town Centre, 150yds; A591, 200yds; M6 jct 36, 15 miles; Ambleside, 4 miles

Attractions: Exclusive Boat Charter on Lake Windermere; Lake District National Park; Beatrix Potter Centre; Brockhole Visitor Centre and Holehird Gardens

A truly rare find, this small Lake District hotel is a warm and cosy country home built in 1891 by the pioneer Lakeland hotelier John Rigg. Close to the centre of Windermere, some rooms have views towards the village whilst others overlook the stunning Lakeland Fells. Each of the bedrooms is elegantly and individually furnished with features such as mood lighting, wall mounted LCD TVs and quality Egyptian cotton bedding. For a particularly indulgent stay, reserve the Luxury Room with huge jet whirlpool bath and chromatherapy lighting or the Superior Room fitted with a 7-foot wide bed! Escape and relax after a day's walking beside the roaring fire in the oak-panelled bar and enjoy a pre-dinner glass of wine or local real ale on the terrace in warmer weather. Then head to the highly acclaimed Villa Restaurant, where Head Chef John Kelly presents diverse dishes created from the best local produce including "Fell bred" steaks and Cumberland smoked cheese.

CEDAR MANOR HOTEL

AMBLESIDE ROAD, WINDERMERE, CUMBRIA LA23 1AX
Tel: 015394 43192 **International:** +44 (0)15394 43192
Web: www.condenastjohansens.com/cedarmanor **E-mail:** info@cedarmanor.co.uk

"Lovely room, wonderful food, the perfect place to relax." This is just one of the many comments in the guest book of this charming and picturesque country house hotel set in the heart of the Lake District. The Gothic-styled Cedar Manor Hotel, with its solid grey stone outer walls, grey slated roof and tall arched windows, is a former Victorian gentleman's retreat ½ mile from Windermere town centre. Thanks to owners Jonathan and Caroline Kaye it is now a stylish and relaxing home-from-home with 11 delightfully elegant bedrooms. Each room is furnished with locally crafted pieces and some have views over the Lake and Langdale Pikes. Spoil yourself and stay in The Coach House Suite with its light and airy lounge and super king-size bed, or in the Langdale room, which features a king-size canopy bed plus spa bath. And be sure to dine at the highly acclaimed restaurant whose seasonally changing menus have become a local attraction.

Our inspector loved: The friendly and relaxing atmosphere at this small, informal Lake District hotel with excellent food.

Price Guide:
single £90-£130
double £110-£150
suite £180-£350

Awards/Recognition: 2 AA Rosettes 2011-2012

Location: A591, 10 yards; M6 jct 36, 17 miles; Windermere Town Centre, 0.5 miles; Windermere Station, 0.25 miles

Attractions: Windermere Town and Lake; Blackwell Arts & Crafts House; Beatrix Potter Centre; Dove Cottage

THE WINDERMERE SUITES

NEW ROAD, WINDERMERE, CUMBRIA LA23 2LA
Tel: 015394 44739 **International:** +44 (0)15394 44739
Web: www.condenastjohansens.com/windermeresuites **E-mail:** pureluxury@windermeresuites.co.uk

Our inspector loved: This luxurious and romantic retreat with its avant garde décor.

Price Guide:
single from £150
suite £195-£320

Location: Windermere Town Centre, 500yds; Lake Windermere, 1 mile; A591, 0.5 miles; M6 Jct 36, 14 miles

Attractions: Lake District National Park; Beatrix Potter Museum; Blackwell Arts & Crafts; National Trust Properties

The Windermere Suites is not your average 5-star boutique accommodation but an original and sophisticated all suite property with an emphasis on romance and relaxation. This is the perfect destination for honeymooners or hopeless romantics, where each spacious suite is guaranteed to surpass your expectations. Fitted with modern designer furniture and lavish bathrooms with oversized double airbath, underfloor heating and Chromotherapy mood lighting, each suite also has its very own lounge area with wall-mounted TV. A plentiful Cumbrian platter or Continental breakfast is brought to you each day and a room service menu of drinks and snacks is available until 10pm. In addition, a chauffeur service to and from Holbeck Ghyll's Michelin-Starred restaurant, for lunches and evening meals, can be arranged. Just a 2-minute walk from Windermere Village and a stroll away from Bowness, there are plenty of sights, shops, restaurants and bars to enjoy close by.

FAYRER GARDEN HOUSE HOTEL

LYTH VALLEY ROAD, BOWNESS-ON-WINDERMERE, CUMBRIA LA23 3JP
Tel: 015394 88195 **International:** +44 (0)15394 88195
Web: www.condenastjohansens.com/fayrergarden **E-mail:** lakescene@fayrergarden.com

Our inspector loved: *Dining in the air-conditioned restaurant with panoramic views of Lake Windermere.*

Price Guide: (including 5-course dinner)
single £85–£140
standard £150–£210
lake view £214–£300

Location: A5074, 0.25 miles; A591, 8 miles; M6 jct 36, 16 miles; Windermere, 2.5 miles

Attractions: Lake Windermere; Lake District National Park and Visitor Centre; Beatrix Potter; Blackwell Arts and Crafts House

Fayrer Garden House Hotel is a lovely Victorian house in spacious gardens and grounds. A sophisticated hotel and restaurant that boasts wonderful views of Lake Windermere, offering excellent value for money for its sumptuous food, fine wines and high standard of friendly yet professional service. The garden is full of gorgeous colours and a terrace enviably positioned to catch all the afternoon sun. Menus change daily and use local produce such as fish, game and poultry – whatever is in season. The wine list is excellent and again, very reasonably priced. Many of the bedrooms benefit from the views, some with four-posters and some leading directly onto the garden. There is much to entertain you nearby, with guests having complimentary use of nearby spa and leisure facilities, boating from Bowness Pier, golf at Windermere Golf Club and The Beatrix Potter attraction amongst the favourites. Hotel closed 1st week of January.

BROADOAKS COUNTRY HOUSE

BRIDGE LANE, TROUTBECK, WINDERMERE, CUMBRIA LA23 1LA
Tel: 01539 445566 **International:** +44 (0)1539 445566
Web: www.condenastjohansens.com/broadoaks **E-mail:** info@broadoakscountryhouse.co.uk

***Our inspector loved:** This charming secluded hotel with beautiful views over the Troutbeck Valley yet only 5 minutes from Windermere.*

Price Guide:
single £70–£160
double £90–£230

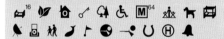

Location: M6 jct 36, 18 miles; A591, 0.5 mile; Windermere, 1.5 miles; Ambleside, 4 miles

Attractions: Lake District National Park; Lake Windermere; Beatrix Potter Centre; Brockhole Visitors Centre & Holehead Gardens

A striking vista across the Troutbeck Valley and Lake Windermere makes Broadoaks a delightful retreat for those exploring the picturesque Lake District. At this special hotel you will find warm English hospitality, period styling, personal touches luxury accommodation and many impressive original features. Furnishings in the bedrooms are mindful of the graceful building's Victorian past, some featuring four-poster or antique brass bedsteads. A favourite room is the elegant music room complete with Bechstein piano, an open fireplace and barrel vaulted ceiling. Here you can enjoy a pre-dinner cocktail before dinner in the light and elegant dining room. Daily and signature dishes show creativity for winning combinations of seasonal textures, tastes and flavours. This secluded hotel with is spectacular views is just the sort of place you can curl up with a good book or enjoy outside pursuits such as fishing and clay pigeon shooting in the grounds.

HOLMEFIELD COUNTRY GUEST HOUSE

DALE ROAD NORTH, DARLEY DALE, NEAR BAKEWELL, MATLOCK, DERBYSHIRE DE4 2HY
Tel: 01629 735347 **International:** +44 (0)1629 735347
Web: www.condenastjohansens.com/holmefield **E-mail:** holmefieldguesthouse@btinternet.com

Set in the glorious Peak District National Park, Holmefield is a carefully restored Victorian home and coach house with 5 AA Star highly commended accommodation and locally supplied restaurant. Between Bakewell and Matlock, just a 5-minute drive from Chatsworth and Haddon Hall, the property is surrounded by an acre of its own gardens and grounds. The views over Derwent Valley and historic Peak Rail steam trains are picture-perfect. Owners Kate and Geoff provide a personalised service that goes above and beyond expectations. Their en-suite bedrooms are located in both the main house and the coach house; each unique in style and characterful. Guests may unwind in the sitting room by the open fire with a complimentary glass of sherry before adjourning to the dining room where original mouldings and cornices have been retained. Meals are skilfully prepared from produce much of which is grown and reared on a nearby farm.

Our inspector loved: *Looking out over Derwent Valley and the Peak Rail steam trains.*

Price Guide:
single £79-£130
double £95-£132

Location: A6, 10yds; Matlock, 3 miles; Bakewell, 4 miles; Chesterfield, 12 miles

Attractions: Chatsworth; Haddon Hall; Peak Rail's Preserved Railway and Steam Trains; Peak District National Park

THE CARY ARMS

BABBACOMBE BEACH, SOUTH DEVON TQ1 3LX
Tel: 01803 327110 **International:** +44 (0)1803 327110
Web: www.condenastjohansens.com/caryarms **E-mail:** enquiries@caryarms.co.uk

Our inspector loved: *The tucked away location and warm hospitality of this contemporary seafront inn.*

Price Guide:
deluxe £160-£200
luxury £220-£260
suite £310-£360

Awards/Recognition: Condé Nast Johansens Most Excellent Inn 2011

Location: A379, 0.5 miles; A380, 12 miles; M5/Exeter, 22 miles; Newton Abbot, 10 miles

Attractions: Babbacombe Cliff Railway; Cockington Court; Torre Abbey; Green Way - Former Home of Agatha Christie

The Cary Arms is all about dazzling sea views and the values of good English inns matched with the style and comfort of a high spec luxury boutique hotel. As we have come to expect from the innovative enterprises of Peter de Savary this is a true gem standing serenely on the water's edge close to the village of Babbacombe. Beamed ceilings, aged floorboards, stone walls, books, board games and plenty of character has been meticulously pulled together. Big and airy bedrooms combine comfort with seaside chic that includes Italian bed linens, bespoke fabrics and huge bathrooms. After a busy beach day or a stirring coastal walk, there's little to better the Cary's crab sandwich or locally sourced John Dory fillet washed down with a glass of fine wine taken inside or out on the terrace. Dine al fresco on the terraces and around the garden-side fireplace. Pampering is available in the Elemis Spa Room, products are designed to treat the skin with powerful results.

THE HAMPTON'S HOTEL

EXCELSIOR VILLAS, TORRS PARK, ILFRACOMBE, DEVON EX34 8AZ
Tel: 01271 864246 **International:** +44 (0)1271 864246
Web: www.condenastjohansens.com/hamptonshotel **E-mail:** info@thehamptonshotel.com

Our inspector loved: *The beautiful design and far reaching views from this terrific boutique hotel.*

Price Guide:
standard double £70-£85
luxury double £85-£100
junior suite £120-£140

Location: Tunnels Beaches, 0.5 miles; Croyde, 9 miles; Saunton Sands, 10 miles; Woolacombe, 6 miles

Attractions: Ilfracombe Theatre and Museum; Exmoor; Lundy Island; Surfing

Elevated high with far-reaching views over the town of Ilfracombe and beyond to the sea, the family run Hampton's is a chic boutique style hotel located within Victorian villas. A perfect base for enjoying North Devon's coastal walks, surf, sea life, rock pools, golf and local food, this superbly designed getaway is ideal for families and couples alike. Offering the best in comfort and indulgence, The Hampton's provides hotel luxury for bed and breakfast prices and prides itself on attention to detail. This is no more evident than in the bedrooms, which were decorated by an award-winning designer. Each bedroom has a distinct personality yet all feature Egyptian cotton sheets, flat-screen TVs, DVD players and free WiFi access. Evening meals can be arranged for six or more diners and the spacious living room can accommodate up to 14 for a dinner party. The inviting lounge area with log fire, is a cosy spot to enjoy a film from the extensive DVD library.

THE OLD RECTORY HOTEL

MARTINHOE, EXMOOR NATIONAL PARK, DEVON EX31 4QT
Tel: 01598 763368 **International:** +44 (0)1598 763368
Web: www.condenastjohansens.com/oldrectoryexmoor **E-mail:** info@oldrectoryhotel.co.uk

Our inspector loved: *The great location, excellent food and comfortable rooms. All you could wish for.*

Price Guide:
double £210
suite £245

Awards/Recognition: Condé Nast Johansens Taittinger Wine List Award, Special Commendation Best Newcomer 2011; Michelin 1 red Pavilion 2011

Location: South West coastal path, 0.1 miles; Lynmouth, 4 miles; Woolacombe, 12 miles; Barnstaple, 16 miles

Attractions: Exmoor; Various National Trust properties; RHS Rosemore; Lundy Island

Set amidst 3 acres of gardens surrounded by National Trust land, high up on the cliffs of Exmoor National Park, this charming country house retreat is a true gem. Originally a Georgian Rectory, the house has been beautifully and sympathetically refurbished while offering all modern comforts. Each of the 10 individually decorated bedrooms have delightful views, and come filled with thoughtful touches such as Molton Brown toiletries. Dinner at the Old Rectory is a culinary delight, with excellent dishes using local seasonal produce and complemented by wines from the cellar. The garden offers a wonderful tranquil setting with access to the Coastal Path, boasting some of the most spectacular scenery in England. Sit and relax under the 200 year old grape vine in the vinery and watch the local wildlife, take a stroll along the grounds babbling brook and its small waterfalls, or venture into the small Victorian maze.

KINGSTON HOUSE

STAVERTON, NEAR TOTNES, DEVON TQ9 6AR
Tel: 01803 762 235 **International:** +44 (0)1803 762 235
Web: www.condenastjohansens.com/kingstonhouse **E-mail:** info@kingston-estate.co.uk

Our inspector loved: *The warm welcome and homely feel of this small but beautiful country house.*

Price Guide:
single £110–£120
double £190
suite £190–£200

Awards/Recognition: VistEngland–Enjoy English Breakfast Award 2010

Location: A384, 2 miles; A38, 5.5 miles; M5 jct 31, 24 miles; Totnes, 4 miles

Attractions: Exeter; Dartmoor National Park; River Dart; Dartmouth

Offering some of the dreamiest accommodation in the country, the Kingston private estate nestles amongst rolling hills and valleys, bounded by Dartmoor and the sea. Kingston House and its superb self catering holiday cottages have been restored by the Corfields without losing a drop of 18th-century charm. In the main house 3 striking period suites are reached by one of the finest examples of a marquetry staircase in England. The bedrooms have original panelling and shutters, fine plasterwork and profusion of wall paintings. Soak up the atmosphere of crackling log fires in winter, summer drinks on the terrace, and candlelight glittering on sparkling crystal in the elegant dining room. Here you are as welcome as if it were Elizabeth and Michael Corfields' own private house party. Plenty of flexible space for weddings, meetings and gatherings.

THE HORN OF PLENTY HOTEL & RESTAURANT

GULWORTHY, TAVISTOCK, DEVON PL19 8JD
Tel: 01822 832528 **International:** +44 (0)1822 832528
Web: www.condenastjohansens.com/thehornofplenty **E-mail:** info@thehornofplenty.co.uk

Our inspector loved: *The elegant and extensive grounds, and award-winning restaurant.*

Price Guide:
single from £85
double/twin from £95
superior from £195

Awards/Recognition: 2 AA Rosettes 2010-2011

Location: Just off A390; A386, 3.5 miles; A30, 15 miles; Plymouth, 17 miles

Attractions: Dartmoor National Park; Buckland Abbey; Devon Coastline; The Eden Project

This enchanting and refined country house hotel is set in 5 acres of gardens with breathtaking views of natural beauty across the Tamar Valley. Whether you are food lovers looking for fine dining or simply yearning for a luxury break, The Horn of Plenty, with its award-winning restaurant and charming ambience, will not disappoint. Guest rooms are individually styled, with those in the main house classic in character and the garden rooms more contemporary. All feature beautiful fabrics and furnishings, Vi Spring beds and fluffy robes. The restaurant is truly passionate about creating superb food and has gained a renowned reputation for being one of the best restaurants in Devon, if not the South West. Sourcing seasonal produce locally whenever possible, the kitchen creates menus that often include Newlyn crab, rump of Devonshire lamb and Cornish turbot. For a bespoke, truly memorable wedding, look no further!

41

The Grange at Oborne

OBORNE, NEAR SHERBORNE, DORSET DT9 4LA

Tel: 01935 813463 **International:** +44 (0)1935 813463

Web: www.condenastjohansens.com/grangesherborne **E-mail:** reception@thegrange.co.uk

Our inspector loved: The beautiful village setting, friendly welcome and comfortable rooms.

Price Guide:
single from £87
double from £101
four-poster from £143

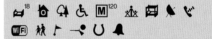

This is a haven from city life where guests can unwind with a fishing trip or relaxed break that simply takes in the local scenery. A 200-year-old house, it nestles peacefully in formal gardens, just 1.5 miles from historic Sherborne. Expect a warm welcome from owners Jennifer and Jon Fletcher and a relaxing ambience in each of the 18 well-appointed and spacious bedrooms. Dinner is served in a most pleasant atmosphere overlooking the attractive floodlit gardens. And thanks to Head Chef Nick Holt's hard work and creativity, the restaurant's international and traditional menu has recently been awarded a second AA Rosette. If planning an event, function for a special occasion, conference or business meeting, the hotel can accommodate up to 120 guests.

Awards/Recognition: 2 AA Rosette 2011-2012

Location: A30, 0.25 mile; M27 jct 2, 45 miles; Sherborne, 1.5 miles; Bristol, 54 miles

Attractions: Stourhead House and Gardens; Stonehenge; The Cerne Abbas Giant; Shaftesbury;

PIER VIEW

5 ROYAL TERRACE, SOUTHEND-ON-SEA, ESSEX SS1 1DY
Tel: 01702 437 900 **International:** +44 (0)1702 437 900
Web: www.condenastjohansens.com/pierview **E-mail:** info@pierviewguesthouse.co.uk

Our inspector loved: *The welcoming atmosphere and panoramic sea views from the Princess Caroline room.*

Price Guide:
single from £58
double from £80
suite £130
exclusive use on request

Location: Overlooking The Pier; Southend Central Train Station, 5-min walk, Southend Victoria Train Station, 10-15 min walk; Southend Central Bus Station, 5-min walk; Southend Airport, 3.5 miles; A127, 3 miles

Attractions: Southend-on-Sea Pier Museum; Adventure Island; The Beach; Cliffs Pavilion

The Georgian Grade II listed Pier View offers exceptionally comfortable guest accommodation in the conversation area of Southend-on-Sea overlooking the seafront and world's longest pleasure pier. Owners, Ed and Barbara Findlay have plenty of hospitality experience behind them and understand that it is the small details that make all the difference. It's not only the luxury linen, WiFi access, flat-screen TVs, original features such as Georgian fireplaces, books and individual design elements but also the care they give to ensure each guest is well looked after during their stay. Light and elegant bedrooms are all named after illustrious visitors to Southend including Lord Nelson and Sir William Heygate, the Lord Mayor of London who proposed the town's first wooden pier. Breakfast is an extensive Continental spread served in the bright seafront room. And in the evening, enjoy a glass of wine before heading out for dinner nearby.

The Swan Hotel

BIBURY, GLOUCESTERSHIRE GL7 5NW

Tel: 01285 740695 **International:** +44 (0)1285 740695
Web: www.condenastjohansens.com/swanhotelbibury **E-mail:** info@swanhotel.co.uk

Our inspector loved: The exclusive garden cottages and perfect village setting right next to the river bank.

Price Guide:
deluxe £160-£300
garden cottage £285-£365

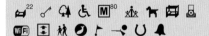

This attractive and enchanting country inn dates back to the 17th century and is set in the heart of Bibury. A great base from which to explore the rolling hills and towns and villages of the Cotswolds, this home from home is nearby Cheltenham and Oxford. Set on the banks of the bubbling River Coln, relax in the pretty landscaped gardens or fish for trout, which the hotel will then cook for you! Whether visiting to fish, romance, get married, celebrate, dine or talk business, this unpretentious, friendly hotel is the ideal retreat. Bedrooms are luxurious with big comfortable beds and lavish bathrooms contain indulgent toiletries. Garden cottages offer exclusivity, private gardens and iPod/MP3 docking stations; one has a hot tub. The award-winning Gallery Restaurant serves stylish modern European-style cuisine and the more informal Café Swan has a courtyard for al fresco lunches, dinners and afternoon tea. The Signet Room is perfect for private dining and larger events.

Awards/Recognition: Condé Nast Johansens Most Excellent Inn Award 2011 Finalist; 1 AA Rosette 2011-2012

Location: A429, 8 miles; M4 jct 15/M5 jct 11, 30 miles; Cheltenham, 17 miles; Birmingham International, 47 miles

Attractions: Bath, Oxford; Touring the Cotswolds; Cotswold Wildlife Park; Bibury Trout Farm

THE WHITE HART ROYAL HOTEL

HIGH STREET, MORETON-IN-MARSH, GLOUCESTERSHIRE GL56 0BA
Tel: 01608 650731 **International:** +44 (0)1608 650731
Web: www.condenastjohansens.com/whitehartroyal **E-mail:** whr@bpcmail.co.uk

Our inspector loved: *The newly refurbished rooms and great village location.*

Price Guide:
standard double/twin £120
feature rooms £160
four poster £160

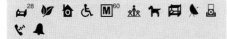

Location: On the A429; Straford-upon-Avon, 10 miles

Attractions: Stratford-upon-Avon; Cotswold Villages; Hidcote Manor Gardens; Snowshill Manor

One night in 1644 King Charles I sheltered here after the battle of Marston Moor, and today, the atmosphere of this handsome sandstone former coaching inn remains as vibrant as its history, making it a fantastic Cotswold hotel. Traditional touches have been retained throughout this Grade II listed property whose 28 individually designed bedrooms include wonderful feature rooms. Many of which, such as the King Charles Suite, have a four-poster bed whilst some boast their very own garden. The converted stable rooms have large wet rooms with roll-top baths, and the American Twin, with 2 double beds, makes an ideal family room. A superb selection of new and old world wines accompanies the delicious menus of predominantly English cuisine with the emphasis firmly on fresh local produce. Fine ales can be savoured by the Snug Bar's inglenook fireplace, in the courtyards' sunshine, or in the comfortable Evesham and Oxford Lounges.

LOWER BROOK HOUSE

BLOCKLEY, NR MORETON-IN-MARSH, GLOUCESTERSHIRE GL56 9DS
Tel: 01386 700286 **International:** +44 (0)1386 700286
Web: www.condenastjohansens.com/lowerbrookhouse **E-mail:** info@lowerbrookhouse.com

Our inspector loved: The tranquil location and comfortable surroundings.

Price Guide:
single £80–£175
double £95–£175

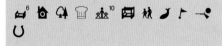

Location: On the B4479; A44, 1.5 miles; Broadway, 8.5 miles

Attractions: Hidcote Manor and Gardens; Snowshill Manor; Sudeley Castle; Broadway Tower

Blockley is a village within a designated Area of Outstanding Natural Beauty and perhaps the ultimate best kept secret of the Cotswolds. Characterised by wisteria covered cottages, dovecotes, and a meandering babbling brook this lovely house, that dates back to the 17th century, stands serenely at its heart. The brook once provided power for 12 mills, 6 of which now give their names to the hotel's charming guest rooms. Owners, Julian and Anna, have taken every care to ensure you feel totally at ease in this idyllic setting. The large, deep open fireplace in the relaxing lounge is a favorite spot for a social chat or just to curl up with a good book. Homemade biscuits in your room, big fluffy bathrobes, sumptuous breakfasts and imaginative dinner menus make this a place you'd like to keep all to yourself.

THREE CHOIRS VINEYARDS ESTATE

NEWENT, GLOUCESTERSHIRE GL18 1LS
Tel: 01531 890223 **International:** +44 (0)1531 890223
Web: www.condenastjohansens.com/threechoirs **E-mail:** info@threechoirs.com

Our inspector loved: The beautiful and unique vineyard setting makes the Three Choirs so much more than just a place to stay.

Price Guide:
standard £115-£145
lodge £145-£175

Awards/Recognition: 2 AA Rosettes 2011-2012

Location: B4215, 2 miles; M5, 5 miles

Attractions: Gloucester; Malvern Hills; Cheltenham; The Dean Heritage Museum

If you are a love of fine wine and gourmet food, then Three Choirs country estate is for you! One of England's best known vineyards, this hidden treasure stands amidst 100 acres of unspoilt countryside and copses. Elegant lodge rooms are perfectly situated between the vines and feature such luxuries as king-size beds, stunning bathrooms and large verandas overlooking the vines. Every little detail is catered for: when you get up in the morning you will find a fresh breakfast hamper delivered to your door and if you would like your own private barbecue, no problem, just ask and all the ingredients will be provided. The award-winning restaurant has a mouth-watering choice of meals and is, of course, complemented by fine wines. Enjoy a stroll around the vineyard and learn a bit about wine-making or sit back and simply immerse yourself in the peaceful surroundings.

THE PIG HOTEL

BEAULIEU ROAD, BROCKENHURST, NEW FOREST, HAMPSHIRE SO42 7QL
Tel: 01590 622354 **International:** +44 (0)1590 622354
Web: www.condenastjohansens.com/thepig **E-mail:** reservations@thepighotel.com

Our inspector loved: *The sumptuous rooms, courtyard dining area and traditional billiards room of this great new hotel.*

Price Guide:
snug £125-£155
comfy £145-£175
spacious £165-£195

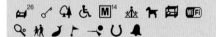

Relaxed, tranquil, interesting and homely, The Pig breaks the mould of designer hotels and presents a style of its own. Quirky elements adorn the muted colour schemed interiors whose shabby chic-inspired décor showcases recycled, restored and reconditioned furnishings. Public rooms have big chairs and sumptuous sofas, roaring fires in winter and a relaxed bar. Truly comfortable and cleverly designed, guest rooms are located in the main house or converted stables and piggery; each offers views of the forest or garden. Outside, hammocks between trees offer further respite. Overseen by Chef James Golding, formerly of The Ivy, Caprice, Sheeky's and Soho House in New York, the constantly changing menus are dictated by ingredients selected by the forager and kitchen gardener, and are therefore full of flavour and inherently faithful to the micro seasons. Try the 15 mile menu that comprises 95% of fresh ingredients sourced from the local area.

Location: B3055, 0.5 miles; Brockenhurst, 2 miles; Lymington, 6.5 miles; London, 90-min drive

Attractions: Exbury Gardens; Lymington Beach; Beaulieu Abbey; Marwell Zoo

THE MILL AT GORDLETON

SILVER STREET, HORDLE, NR LYMINGTON, NEW FOREST, HAMPSHIRE SO41 6DJ
Tel: 01590 682219 **International:** +44 (0)1590 682219
Web: www.condenastjohansens.com/themillatgordleton **E-mail:** info@themillatgordleton.co.uk

Our inspector loved: The wonderful mill stream location, fine food and comfortable rooms.

Price Guide:
single £95–£125
double/twin from £150
balcony £195
main suite £245

Awards/Recognition: Condé Nast Johansens Innovation in Sustainable Hospitality 2009

Location: A337, 2 miles; M27 jct 1, 12 miles; Lymington, 3 miles; Southampton, 23 miles

Attractions: New Forest; Lymington and Harbour; Exbury Gardens; Beaulieu and Bucklers Hard

Cycling holidays, walking holidays and romantic getaways are all made special when staying at this riverside hotel tucked away between the New Forest National Park and sea. This idyllic ivy-clad 17th-century rural hideaway owned and run by Liz Cottingham, who has taken care to immaculately restore it to its former glory. The landscaped gardens exude rustic charm, and visitors weary of their hectic urban lifestyles will certainly relax here to the sound of the mill pond with its charming sluice gates and well-fed ducks. The restaurant has a most welcoming atmosphere and serves an excellent choice of imaginative dishes. On warm sunny days you can sit outside but be sure to book well in advance! The bedrooms have been recently refurbished with delightful bathrooms. The Mill was winner of the Condé Nast Johansens Innovation in Sustainable Hospitality Award 2009.

AYLESTONE COURT

AYLESTONE HILL, HEREFORD, HEREFORDSHIRE HR1 1HS
Tel: 01432 341891 **International:** +44 (0)1432 341891
Web: www.condenastjohansens.com/aylestonecourt **E-mail:** enquiries@aylestonecourt.com

Our inspector loved: Dining in the Orangery overlooking the pretty walled garden.

Price Guide:
single £69–£89
double £85–£118
family from £120

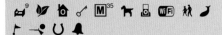

This Grade II listed Georgian town house has been restored and extended to create an inviting, homely environment. The 9 bedrooms are individual and combine original features with modern comforts. Relax in the club style bar or dine in the Georgian restaurant with private dining terrace. Local, seasonal and British dishes are served on all of the menus. The flexible nature of the ground floor rooms means intimate breakfast meetings right through to corporate functions can be well looked after. Two delightful rooms are licensed for civil weddings and are ideal for small meetings and celebrations whilst the walled garden and patio areas provide the perfect backdrop for photographs. Aylestone Court is conveniently located for Hereford's town centre as well as its train station.

Location: On the A4103; A49, 0.5 miles; Hereford Railway Station, 0.5 miles; Town Centre, 1 mile; M50, 10 miles

Attractions: Hereford Cathedral & Mappa Mundi; Hay on Wye; Ludlow; Ross-on-Wye; Ledbury

WILTON COURT

WILTON, ROSS-ON-WYE, HEREFORDSHIRE HR9 6AQ
Tel: 01989 562569 **International:** +44 (0)1989 562569
Web: www.condenastjohansens.com/wiltoncourthotel **E-mail:** info@wiltoncourthotel.com

Our inspector loved: *The award-winning dining that can be enjoyed al fresco on the banks of the River Wye.*

Price Guide:
single £100–£145
double £125–£165
suite £165–£195

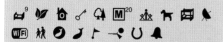

Awards/Recognition: Silver Winner in the Heart of England Excellence in Tourism Awards, Taste of the Heart and Restaurant with Rooms Categories, 2009 and 2010; 2 AA Rosettes 2011-2012

Location: Off the B4260; A40, 0.5 miles; Ross-on-Wye, 0.5 miles; Hereford, 14 miles

Attractions: Wye Valley and Royal Forest of Dean; Hereford Cathedral; Hay-on-Wye; Tintern Abbey

Owners Helen and Roger Wynn were trained under the auspicious eye of renowned quality hotels and this valuable experience is evident in the professional care and personal effort at their 5 Star AA restaurant with rooms. Leaded windows, stone mullions, walled gardens with mature shrubs and sloping lawns down to the River Wye make this a delight. Recently refurbished bedrooms feature lovely views, and the kitchen's 2 Rosette awarded menus can be enjoyed in either the River view Restaurant and Bar with a warming fire in winter or the Mulberry Restaurant with conservatory overlooking the walled gardens. In summer months meals may also be taken al fresco in the courtyard or riverbank. Local activities include walking, canoeing, cycling and fishing. Wilton Court's many accolades include Visit Wales Gold Award since 2008 and it has been a finalist in the Flavours of Herefordshire Awards since 2003.

THE PRIORY BAY HOTEL

PRIORY DRIVE, SEAVIEW, ISLE OF WIGHT PO34 5BU

Tel: 01983 613146 **International:** +44 (0)1983 613146
Web: www.condenastjohansens.com/priorybayiow **E-mail:** enquiries@priorybay.co.uk

Our inspector loved: The terrific ambience created when the hotel is lit by candles, and the private sandy beach.

Price Guide:
single from £70
double £160-£300
suite £300-£375

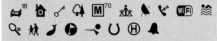

Overlooking the sea from atop a small valley, The Priory Bay Hotel is a Virginia creeper-clad country hideaway, perfect for a luxury break on the Isle of Wight. The private estate is surrounded by no less than 70 acres of tranquil grounds including woodland teeming with wildlife and birds of prey. Guests enter the hotel via a beautifully carved medieval arched stone entrance and into public rooms framed by tall windows and heavy curtains. Each bedroom is comfortable, and individually furnished with views of the grounds or sea. And there are 2 restaurants to choose from, one of which is fine dining while the other is a brasserie-style venue with terrace. Both showcase superb British cuisine with a contemporary twist. Furthermore, there is an outdoor pool, adjoining 6-hole golf course, tennis courts, falconry classes, surrounding woodlands and flower-filled gardens to enjoy. Coastal paths pass by the gate, and beyond the woods is the private, secluded beach.

Awards/Recognition: 1 AA Rosette 2011-2012

Location: A3055, 2 miles; Ryde, 3.5 miles; Cowes (Southampton) Ferry Terminal, 10.6 miles; Fishbourne (Portsmouth) Ferry Terminal, 6.1 miles

Attractions: Ventnor Botanic Garden; Osborne House; Carisbrooke Castle; Sailing at Seaview and Bembridge

RYLSTONE MANOR

RYLSTONE GARDENS, SHANKLIN, ISLE OF WIGHT PO37 6RG
Tel: 01983 862806 **International:** +44 (0)1983 862806
Web: www.condenastjohansens.com/rylstonemanor **E-mail:** rylstone.manor@btinternet.com

Our inspector loved: *The welcoming atmosphere, attention to detail and fabulous food.*

Price Guide: (including dinner)
single £75–£110
double £140–£230

Awards/Recognition: Condé Nast Johansens Most Excellent Value 2009

Location: A3055, 0.25 mile; Shanklin, 0.5 mile; Cowes (Southampton) Ferry Terminal, 12 miles; Fishbourne (Portsmouth) Ferry Terminal, 10 miles

Attractions: Osborne House; Ventnor Botanic Gardens; Godshill Old Village; Carisbrooke Castle

Carole and Michael Hailston are the proud owners of Rylstone Manor, a delightful manor house hotel hidden away in 4½ acres of tranquil mature gardens on the edge of Shanklin, perfect for a break to the Isle of Wight. You can catch a glimpse of the sea from some of the charming bedrooms and the stylish day rooms are just the thing for a good book and afternoon tea. Of course in good weather you will probably wish to be outside for much of the day and from the clifftop you will be able to enjoy stunning views of Shanklin Bay and a 2-minute walk leads to the promenade and beach. The restaurant menu changes daily and is complemented by a well thought out wine list which includes some interesting local vintages.

Wallett's Court Hotel & Spa

WEST CLIFFE, ST MARGARET'S-AT-CLIFFE, DOVER, KENT CT15 6EW
Tel: 01304 852424 **International:** +44 (0)1304 852424
Web: www.condenastjohansens.com/wallettscourt **E-mail:** mail@wallettscourt.com

Our inspector loved: The great mix of Jacobean and contemporary features that create great interest at every turn.

Price Guide:
single £109–£139
double £129–£169
suite £199

Awards/Recognition: 2 AA Rosettes 2011-2012

Location: A2, 1 mile; M2 jct7, 30 miles; Dover, 3 miles; Gatwick Airport, 73 miles

Attractions: Dover Castle; White Cliffs of Dover; Canterbury Cathedral; Leeds Castle; St Margaret's Bay Beach; Bay Trust Gardens

This grade 2 listed manor house hotel was found in ruins during the late 1970s by the Oakley family, who thankfully picked it up and put it back on its feet. In the main house the Jacobean staircase leads to one of the three traditional four poster bedrooms and across the courtyard there are 17 rooms decorated in contemporary design housed in converted Kentish hay barns. On top of excellent hospitality there is a spa complete with hydrotherapy pool and treatment cabins set in the woods and the latest attraction - a real red indian tipi complete with double bed. The restaurant is deservedly popular locally and local ingredients are important - try the St Margaret's Bay lobster or Romney Marsh lamb. You can practice clay pigeon shooting with a professional or have a round of golf atop the White Cliffs or simply relax here for a day or two before heading over to France.

LITTLE SILVER COUNTRY HOTEL

ASHFORD ROAD, ST MICHAELS, TENTERDEN, KENT TN30 6SP
Tel: 01233 850321 **International:** +44 (0)1233 850321
Web: www.condenastjohansens.com/littlesilver **E-mail:** enquiries@little-silver.co.uk

Our inspector loved: *The friendly service and welcoming atmosphere.*

Price Guide:
single from £62
double/twin from £97
suites from £160

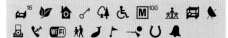

Location: On the A28; M20 jct 9, 12 miles; Tenterden, 0.5 miles; Gatwick Airport, 52 miles

Attractions: Sissinghurst and Great Dixter Gardens; Ancient Rye; Leeds and Bodiam Castles; Canterbury Cathedral

An unexpected find in the Weald of Kent, this wood framed Tudor-style hotel welcomes you with friendly hospitality and excellent service. An idyllic choice for a weekend getaway as well as longer breaks, wedding receptions and celebrations. Especially attractive is the Kentish oast-house inspired octagonal hall with stained-glass windows, which can accommodate up to 150 guests. The beamed lounge's blazing log fires bring warmth and pleasure to a grey winter's day. Individually furnished bedrooms and suites deliver complete comfort, some with four-poster beds, Spa baths, and views across the gardens. 2 rooms are particularly suitable for wheelchair users. Good food is never far away, with breakfast, morning coffee, lunch, afternoon tea and dinner served in the Oaks restaurant.

FERRARI'S RESTAURANT & HOTEL

THORNLEY, LONGRIDGE, PRESTON, LANCASHIRE PR3 2TB
Tel: 01772 783148 **International:** +44 (0)1772 783148
Web: www.condenastjohansens.com/ferraris **E-mail:** info@ferrariscountryhouse.co.uk

Our inspector loved: The Italian hospitality and friendliness at this family run hotel.

Price Guide:
single £50–£110
double/twin £70–£130

Location: B5269, 1.5 miles; M6 jct 31a, 15-min drive; Longridge, 1.5 miles; Preston, 25-min drive

Attractions: Ribble Valley; Clitheroe; Preston; Blackpool

This impressive Lancashire hotel and resturant is located in the tranquil Ribble Valley with fine food and superb hospitality in abundance. One of the finest West Midlands hotels around and idyllic wedding locations the house was originlly built by the Earl of Derby in 1830 as a shooting lodge. Today it's a family owned affair, with Susan Ferrari and daughter Luisa overseeing the kitchen and restaurant. Dishes are a combination of traditional English and Italian cooking, including loin of Lamb of rosemary and Insalata di Gamberi. The Ferraris pride themselves on a personalised wedding service, working together with each couple to provide the perfect day. Comfortable bedrooms are individually styled, some have Jacuzzis and half-tester Tudor beds, and many feature antique furniture and garden views. You're spoilt for choice with places to visit as the historic market town of Clitheroe and its famous Norman castle are on the doorstep, as well as the natural beauty of rural Lancashire.

THE OLD RECTORY

103 YARMOUTH ROAD, NORWICH, NORFOLK NR7 0HF
Tel: 01603 700772 **International:** +44 (0)1603 700772
Web: www.condenastjohansens.com/oldrectorynorwich **E-mail:** enquiries@oldrectorynorwich.com

Our inspector loved: *The homely atmosphere and mix of old and modern between the light and airy coach house rooms and the traditional rectory.*

Price Guide:
single £95-£125
double £125-£160

Awards/Recognition: 2 AA Rosettes 2011-2012

Location: A47, 2 miles; Norwich, 2 miles; Norwich Airport, 4 miles

Attractions: Whitlingham Country Park; Norwich Cathedral; Sandringham

The promise of a warm welcome and personal service will draw you to this wisteria-clad grade 2 listed Georgian house. Set in an acre of mature gardens on the outskirts of Norwich overlooking the Yare Valley the spacious bedrooms and elegant Drawing Room offer a great place to relax. The award-winning dinner menu changes daily and in the summer months includes fresh produce from the hotels own gardens. The tempting English breakfast features sausages, bacon and ham from local farmers Barnards of Shropham as well as milk from Norton's Dairy and Chef James' own toasted muesli and fruit compote. If you must talk business the Wellingtonia Room and Conservatory, overlooking the pool terrace and gardens, provide a unique venue for small meetings. To escape, the Dowagers Cottage in the grounds is a comfortable self-contained option.

WAREN HOUSE HOTEL

WAREN MILL, BAMBURGH, NORTHUMBERLAND NE70 7EE

Tel: 01668 214581 **International:** +44 (0)1668 214581

Web: www.condenastjohansens.com/warenhouse **E-mail:** enquiries@warenhousehotel.co.uk

Our inspector loved: The delicious dinner menu using locally sourced and home grown produce.

Price Guide:
single £90–£151
double £135–£185
suite £168–£236

Set in 6 acres of gardens and woodland on the edge of Budle Bay Bird Sanctuary overlooking Holy Island and close to the majestic Bamburgh Castle and Alnwick Gardens is this pretty Georgian hotel brimming with antique furnishings and immaculate décor that creates a warm ambience. Choose from a daily changing menu and complementary fine wines in the candle-lit dining room surrounded by family portraits. Owners Anita and Peter don't cater for under 14s, so peace and tranquility are assured even in the summer months. Dogs are welcome by prior arrangement. "To visit it the North East and not to stay here, would be foolish indeed", so says one of many complimentary entries in the hotel's visitors' book. This delightful, traditional country house will meet all your expectations. Special breaks are available.

Awards/Recognition: 1 AA Rosette 2010-2011

Location: B1342, 200yds; A1, 2 miles; Bamburgh, 3 miles; Alnwick, 15 miles

Attractions: Bamburgh Castle; Holy Island & Farne Islands; Alnwick Castle & Gardens; Budle Bay Wildlife Sanctuary

COCKLIFFE COUNTRY HOUSE HOTEL

BURNTSTUMP COUNTRY PARK, BURNTSTUMP HILL, ARNOLD, NOTTINGHAMSHIRE NG5 8PQ

Tel: 0115 968 0179 **International:** +44 (0)115 968 0179
Web: www.condenastjohansens.com/cockliffe **E-mail:** enquiries@cockliffehouse.co.uk

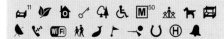

Our inspector loved: *The accessibility of this peaceful, charming small hotel that is so discreetly hidden away.*

Price Guide:
single from £89
double from £109

Awards/Recognition: 1 AA Rosette 2011-2012

Location: A614, 2 miles; M1 jct 26, 9 miles; Nottingham, 7 miles; East Midlands Airport, 23 miles

Attractions: Nottingham Castle; Sherwood Forest; Southwell Minster; Newstead Abbey

For those who have never found Cockliffe Country House nor sought it out, you may be surprised to discover that it has sat secluded from the hustle and bustle of both Nottingham and Mansfield for over 300 years, yet is perfectly located for visiting Nottingham Castle, Southwell Minster, Newstead Abbey and Sherwood Forest. It is hard to imagine a rustic idyll nestling peacefully, yet conveniently, between the A60 and A614 but seemingly miles from anywhere. Owners Dane and Jane Clarke became enchanted by this secret hideaway 16 years ago and have combined their flair for innovative style and cuisine. Each bedroom has its own personality nurtured by Jane's use of fabric, antiques and colour, and the resolute approach to the customer as an individual is a quality rarely found in many hotels. With its alluring ambience and gastronomy nurtured by a talented team, whose skills were gained in Michelin-Starred kitchens, Cockliffe leaves a lasting impression.

GREENWOOD LODGE

5 THIRD AVENUE, SHERWOOD RISE, NOTTINGHAM NG7 6JH
Tel: 0115 962 1206 **International:** +44 (0)115 962 1206
Web: www.condenastjohansens.com/greenwoodlodge **E-mail:** info@greenwoodlodgecityguesthouse.co.uk

Our inspector loved: The antique four poster beds and the delicious breakfast served in the conservatory.

Price Guide:
single £47.50–£60
double £75–£95

Location: City Centre, 1 mile; A610, 2 miles; M1 jct 26, 6 miles; East Midlands Airport, 30-min drive

Attractions: Nottingham Castle & Robin Hood; Lace Market; Theatre; National Arena Ice Rink

This home from home enjoys a quiet, secluded location in the heart of a conservation area, yet is conveniently just 1 mile from Nottingham city centre. Built in 1834, the lodge is set in a mature courtyard garden, filled with lovingly tended shrubs and trees. Immaculately maintained throughout, the lodge features antique furniture and paintings and retains a sense of traditional refinement as well as home-from-home charm. The attractive rooms are individually decorated in fresh colour schemes and feature antique furniture and paintings. Three feature striking four poster beds. A notable breakfast menu is served in the airy conservatory and whilst lunch and dinner are not provided a delicious afternoon tea is available. Of course you may just be happy to curl up in the beautiful lounge with a drink and a good book.

BURFORD HOUSE

99 HIGH STREET, BURFORD, OXFORDSHIRE OX18 4QA
Tel: 01993 823151 **International:** +44 (0)1993 823151
Web: www.condenastjohansens.com/burfordhouse **E-mail:** stay@burfordhouse.co.uk

Our inspector loved: The great and very convenient location, welcoming atmosphere and attention to detail.

Price Guide: (room only)
single from £124
double from £179
joining family suite upon request

Location: A40, 0.5 miles; M40, 15 miles; Oxford, 21 miles; Heathrow Airport, 62 miles

Attractions: Oxford; Blenheim Palace; Hidcote Manor Garden; Sudeley Castle

A handsome 17th-century townhouse hotel on a Cotswold stone high street, Burford House is a home from home, well loved by its owners and guests. Ian Hawkins and Stewart Dunkley provide excellent service and welcome you to their hotel whose dedicated, local staff have worked here for many years. Highly Commended by the AA with 5 Yellow Stars, this elegant retreat exudes a truly lovely atmosphere, and features bedrooms decorated in classic Farrow & Ball hues filled with antique furniture, sumptuous beds, linens and gleaming bathrooms with plenty of character. Stewart's delicious menus use the finest in local organic produce available, to create fantastic breakfasts - recipient of the AA's Breakfast Award - and afternoon teas in one of 2 intimate sitting rooms. Dine Monday-Saturday with a 2 or 3-course light lunch in the dining room or al fresco in the courtyard. Dinner on Thursday, Friday and Saturday evenings is also available.

THE LAMB INN

SHEEP STREET, BURFORD, OXFORDSHIRE OX18 4LR
Tel: 01993 823155 **International:** +44 (0)1993 823155
Web: www.condenastjohansens.com/lambinnburford **E-mail:** info@lambinn-burford.co.uk

Our inspector loved: The rustic charm of the bar area combines beautifully with the contemporary yet traditional bedrooms.

Price Guide:
single £120-£170
double £155-£250
suite £210-£275

Walk into the picture perfect Lamb Inn and instantly recapture something of the 14th century. Flagged floors, antiques, and the flicker of log fires on gleaming copper, brass and silver. Cleverly amongst the traditional elements is a complementary tone of the contemporary, in particular in the stunning Allium suite which adds an indulgent feel. The delicious locally sourced bar meals and the more formal award winning restaurant specialise in fresh fish and in summer you can eat outside in the pretty walled garden. Located near the heart of Burford you might like to browse through antiques shops or laze by the waters of the River Windrush. Within easy reach of Oxford, Cheltenham, Stow-on-the-Wold and other quintessential Cotswold villages. The Lamb can be either for romance, business or as an ideal venue for a house party if getting together with friends or family for a special occasion.

Awards/Recognition: Condé Nast Johansens Most Excellent Inn 2009 Winner and Readers Award 2011 Finalist; Cotswold Life Food and Drink Awards Hotel Restaurant of the Year 2011 Highly Commended; 2 AA Rosettes 2011-2012

Location: A40, 1 mile; M40, 20 miles; Burford, 30yds; Birmingham Airport, 50 miles

Attractions: Cotswold Tours; Cheltenham Racecourse; Cotswold Wildlife Park; Sherbourne Estate(NT)

OLD SWAN & MINSTER MILL

MINSTER LOVELL, NEAR BURFORD, OXFORDSHIRE OX29 0RN
Tel: 01993 774441 **International:** +44 (0)1993 774441
Web: www.condenastjohansens.com/milloldswan **E-mail:** enquiries@oldswanandminstermill.com

Our inspector loved: The rooms overlooking the village stream with their own terraces and cosy outdoor fires.

Price Guide:
cosy £165
special £225
luxe £250
suite £325

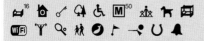

Location: A40, 2.5 miles; Oxford, 15 miles; M40 jct 8 and 9, 20 miles; Cheltenham, 26 miles

Attractions: Blenheim Palace; Cheltenham Racecourse; Cotswold Wildlife Park and Gardens; Sudeley Castle and Gardens; Stratford-Upon-Avon

Oak beams, log fires and the charm of bygone years create the perfect Cotswolds hotel at the Old Swan. Set alongside the bubbling waters of the River Windrush, this is the ideal, quintessential English spot to escape, explore and unwind. The 16 guest rooms and suites are relaxed and romantic, with luxurious fabrics, modern bathrooms and conveniences. Some overlook the gardens and meadows beyond. With a laid-back gastro-pub atmosphere in the dining room and cosy bar, you can enjoy superb, fresh local ingredients, crafted into hearty dishes. The cathedral-style Big Dining Room is also available for up to 60 guests privately. Canine companions are also made to feel welcome at the Old Swan. For a small charge they are invited to stay with you in allocated rooms, with dog bowls and beds awaiting their arrival. Wonderful walks abound throughout the surrounding area, for dogs and owners alike!

The Nut Tree Pub

MURCOTT, KIDLINGTON, OXFORDSHIRE OX5 2RE
Tel: 01865 331253 **International:** +44 (0)1865 331253
Web: www.condenastjohansens.com/nuttreeinn

Our inspector loved: Michael North's incredible cuisine, and the welcoming atmosphere.

Price Guide:
starters £7.50–£14
main £16.50–£27
dessert £5.50–£7.50
set menu Tues-Fri (lunch) and
Tues-Thurs (evening)
2 course £18; 3 course £22

Awards/Recognition: 1 Michelin Star 2011; 2 AA Rosettes 2011-2012; Best Use of Local Produce Good Food Guide 2010; Caterer & Hotelkeeper, Newcomer of the Year 2009

Location: A34, 6 miles; M40 jct 9, 6 miles; Oxford, 10 miles

Attractions: Oxford; Bicester Shopping Village; Boarstal Duck Decoy; Nature Reserve

The Nut Tree Pub, with its thatched roof and village pond, effortlessly and unaffectedly combines a country pub ambience with the informal sophistication of a great restaurant, ideal for business lunches, private dining, celebrations and wedding receptions. Savour real ale from the cask before sampling the fabulous modern British cuisine created by owner Mike, who has now earnt The Nut Tree Pub a Michelin Star for his wonderfully creative dishes featuring seasonal flavours. The emphasis is uncomplicated but delicious cooking. Dishes include home smoked salmon, homemade breads and ice-cream and succulent meats from The Nut Tree's very own reared pigs. It's also great value with menus starting from £15! During the summer, dine al fresco in the company of the Gloucester Old Spot Tamworth pigs stabled nearby. The staff will happily recommend nearby accommodation.

Pen-Y-Dyffryn Country Hotel

RHYDYCROESAU, NEAR OSWESTRY, SHROPSHIRE SY10 7JD
Tel: 01691 653700 **International:** +44 (0)1691 653700
Web: www.condenastjohansens.com/penydyffryn **E-mail:** stay@peny.co.uk

Our inspector loved: The delicious dinner at this peaceful haven with stunning views of Welsh mountains and Shropshire countryside.

Price Guide:
single from £86
double £115–£190

Awards/Recognition: Condé Nast Johansens Most Excellent Value for money 2011; 2 AA Rosettes 2011-2012

Location: A 5, 4 miles; Oswestry 3 miles; Chester, 28 miles; Shrewsbury, 20 miles

Attractions: Welsh Borders; Lake Vyrnwy; Pistyll Rhaedr Waterfalls; various National Trust properties

Enjoying breathtaking Welsh mountain views from high on the last hill in Shropshire, this captivating Condé Nast Johansens Best Value for Money award-winning hotel, offers you the chance to totally relax and unwind. Built in 1845 as a Georgian rectory for a Celtic scholar, the Grade 2 listed property now happily rests in the hands of owners Miles and Audrey Hunter, who provide a well-established discreet service and cosy atmosphere. All bedrooms, some of which have Jacuzzis or spa baths, overlook the attractive terraced gardens, while 4 rooms in the coach-house have private patios. Chef David Morris - awarded 2 AA Rosettes - creates menus from local, often organic, produce. Peruse the exciting wine list with many organic wines alongside non-alcoholic organic drinks. Chester and Shrewsbury are nearby and the local area offers hill walking, riding, golf, and trout fishing.

SOULTON HALL

NEAR WEM, SHROPSHIRE SY4 5RS
Tel: 01939 232786 **International:** +44 (0)1939 232786
Web: www.condenastjohansens.com/soultonhall **E-mail:** enquiries@soultonhall.co.uk

Our inspector loved: This charming historic hall and family home, and Ann's use of so much of their own produce from the gardens and farm.

Price Guide:
single from £71
double £110–£142
exclusive use from £1,700

A delightful approach precedes your arrival at this manor house hotel through the unspoilt, tranquil Shropshire countryside, over Soulton brook on an ancient stone bridge and up into the estate, which surrounds Soulton Hall. This family run property has exceptional facilities and service that is difficult to beat. Luxury and elegance are words that perfectly describe the interior design, which features stunning antiques and well-preserved architecture that hark back to the Hall's historical roots. Dining is a treat in itself: Ann Ashton is a wonderful cook who uses as much home-grown produce as possible; even the game comes from the area. If you feel like a stroll on their private estate, don't forget to explore the delightful walled gardens, a quiet sanctuary. Soulton Hall offers an extraordinarily peaceful experience, yet is close to the cities of Chester and Shrewsbury.

Location: On the B5065; A49, 2 miles; Shrewsbury, 10 miles; M54 jct 7, 18 miles

Attractions: Chester; Ironbridge Gorge Museum; Castles of North Wales; Hawkstone Country Park

COMPTON HOUSE

TOWNSEND, AXBRIDGE, SOMERSET BS26 2AJ
Tel: 01934 733944 **International:** +44 (0)1934 733944
Web: www.condenastjohansens.com/comptonhouse **E-mail:** info@comptonhse.com

Our inspector loved: The comfortable rooms, homely atmosphere and rural location that make this a wonderful place to stay.

Price Guide:
double (single occupancy) from £85
double/twin from £110

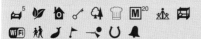

Location: On the A371; M5 jct 21, 10 miles; Bristol, 18.3 miles; Bristol Airport, 9 miles

Attractions: Cheddar Gorge; Wells Cathedral; Bath; Glastonbury

This impressive Grade 2 listed manor house dates back to the 17th-century and is situated in historic Axbridge, at the foot of the Mendip Hills, commanding captivating views over the Somerset Levels to Glastonbury Tor. Surrounded by an expansive and secluded lawned garden, Compton House dates back to Elizabethan times, and oak panelling, elegant mouldings and wonderful fireplaces feature throughout. A great base for numerous walking routes, the hotel has a well-deserved reputation for comfort, hospitality and service, and upholds a continual pursuit of excellence. Its generous bedrooms have many original features, and the attractive dining room serves superb dishes created from Fairtrade and West Country produce. Before enjoying a delicious meal, savour some apèritifs on the sun-catching terrace. Exclusive use for house parties, meetings and weddings can be arranged.

BINHAM GRANGE

OLD CLEEVE, NEAR MINEHEAD, SOMERSET TA24 6HX

Tel: 01984 640056 **International:** +44 (0)1984 640056

Web: www.condenastjohansens.com/binhamgrange **E-mail:** mariethomas@btconnect.com

Our inspector loved: The warm welcome, fantastic food and beautiful gardens. A very special place indeed.

Price Guide:
blue room from £100
abbey room from £140

Location: A39, 1.3 miles; M5 jct 23, 24 miles; Dunster, 4.6 miles; Minehead, 6.5 miles

Attractions: Steam Train to Taunton; Cleeve Abbey; Exmoor; Hestercombe Gardens

As soon as you arrive at this delightful Jacobean farmhouse, you'll find yourself captivated by the sense of total peace and tranquillity. Inside there are many striking original features including an original Jacobean frieze, Tudor alabaster arches and beautiful solid oak doors. The Exmoor Restaurant is a destination in its own right from lunches and teas on the terrace with its far reaching views to dinner served in the Great Hall. Working with the seasons and an extraordinary wealth of local produce Marie and daughter Victoria create delicious menus with occasional hints of their cooking experiences of Italy and Morocco. From your bedroom you can gaze across the beautiful gardens with a traditional orchard that leads to the landscapes beyond. Many little personal touches are dotted around to make you feel welcome, good books to browse through, fresh flowers to brighten up the room and authentic antiques to create a warm, opulent atmosphere.

BOWLISH HOUSE

WELLS ROAD, BOWLISH, SHEPTON MALLET, SOMERSET BA4 5JD
Tel: 01749 342022 **International:** +44 (0)1749 342022
Web: www.condenastjohansens.com/bowlishhouse **E-mail:** info@bowlishhouse.com

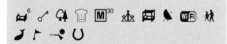

Our inspector loved: *The mix of warm, neutral colours in the recently appointed bedrooms.*

Price Guide:
king room from £80
attic room from £80
four poster from £85

Location: A371, 1-min drive; Castle Cary Station, 10-min drive; Town Centre, 5-min drive

Attractions: Wookey Hole; Wells Cathedral; Roman Baths; Cheddar Gorge

Welcoming and homely, this lovely restaurant with rooms was built in the 18th century and still features many original characteristics that make it worthy of interest, including the Mendip lead drainpipes carrying the crest of the founding owners and a small spring that rises under the cellar. Its comfortable interior is currently being restored to create a natural blend of Georgian architecture alongside muted colour schemes and contemporary art adding a stylish twist. The 6 en-suite bedrooms range from top floor family rooms to first floor double rooms, including one with a four-poster bed. Furthermore, Bowlish House offers a range of well priced, unpretentious menus created from local, freshly prepared produce. Options include à la carte, Early Bird and set lunch and dinner menus.

BERYL

WELLS, SOMERSET BA5 3JP
Tel: 01749 678738 **International:** +44 (0)1749 678738
Web: www.condenastjohansens.com/beryl **E-mail:** stay@beryl-wells.co.uk

Our inspector loved: *There is always a warm welcome at Beryl. The rooms are comfortable the breakfast hearty and the gardens shouldn't be missed.*

Price Guide:
single £75–£95
double £95–£150

This 19th century 5 star mansion is a fine example of gothic architecture, a real little gem set in 13 acres of skilfully restored parkland and gardens. Beryl is tastefully furnished with antiques and offers you hospitality of the highest order. Holly Nowell and her daughter Mary-Ellen are charming hostesses, and take pride in the great attention to detail evident throughout the house. Guests are invited to use the honesty bar in the Green Room or enjoy drinks and wines on the lawn in summer. Holly and Mary-Ellen, who with her husband run a jewellery boutique in the Coach House, are happy to organise group bookings and make reservations for overnight guests at the many first-class restaurants and pubs situated nearby. The bedrooms have interesting views and offer every comfort. A chair lift is available for those that require assistance up to the first floor. Take a dip in Beryl's outdoor pool from May to September.

Location: B3139, 0.36 miles; A371, 2.16 miles; Bath, 21 miles

Attractions: Wells Cathedral; Cheddar Caves & Gorge; Longleat House; Roman Baths

MODDERSHALL OAKS SPA RESTAURANT SUITES

MODDERSHALL, STONE, STAFFORDSHIRE ST15 8TG
Tel: 01782 399000 **International:** +44 (0)1782 399000
Web: www.condenastjohansens.com/moddershalloaks **E-mail:** enquiries@moddershalloaks.com

Our inspector loved: *Being pampered at this peaceful secluded spa in the Staffordshire countryside.*

Price Guide:
single from £120
double from £200

Location: B5066, 500 yards; A520, 1.5 miles; A50, 3 miles; M6 jct 14/15, 10 miles

Attractions: Alton Towers; Trentham Gardens; Staffordshire Potteries

Set in 72 acres of countryside, Moddershall Oaks is a haven set in serene and beautiful surroundings. Exclusive and inspired by the Orient, this is an intimate hotel offering 5 star luxury with just 10 exceptional bedrooms. From the moment you arrive you will feel pampered. The spa facilities are superb and attentive staff are always on hand to make sure your stay is enjoyable. Each suite has outstanding facilities such as under-floor heating, fabulous bathrooms and a soft-seated area. Why not fling open the patio doors and sit on the deck looking out to the beautiful countryside or try the outdoor hot tub, a real indulgence in the heart of Staffordshire. Your taste buds are in for a treat too at the award-winning restaurant! A top team of chefs create modern English dishes through the combination of the freshest seasonal ingredients and local produce. There is also a delightful woodland trail if you feel like exploring.

CLARICE HOUSE

HORRINGER COURT, HORRINGER ROAD, BURY ST EDMUNDS, SUFFOLK IP29 5PH
Tel: 01284 705550 **International:** +44 (0)1284 705550
Web: www.condenastjohansens.com/clarice **E-mail:** bury@claricehouse.co.uk

*Our inspector loved: The relaxed atmosphere
and opportunity to feel totally pampered.*

Price Guide:
single £70–£140
double/twin £120–£160

SPA

Awards/Recognition: 1 AA Rosette 2011-2012

Location: On the A143; A14, 2.3 miles

Attractions: Cambridge; Ely; Newmarket
Racecourse

Clarice House is a residential spa with luxury accommodation within a beautifully refurbished neo-Jacobean mansion set in 20 acres of Suffolk countryside and ancient woodland. The excellent restaurant is open to residents and non-residents, and for those choosing to stay for bed and breakfast, the bedrooms are comfortable and well appointed. A variety of spa break packages include dinner and full use of the spa facilities. A 20-metre indoor swimming pool leads into a spa bath, steam room and sauna. The suite of beauty treatment rooms offers a wide range of indulgent therapies from more traditional to holistic methods such as reflexology, Reiki and Indian head massage.

THE CORNWALLIS COUNTRY HOTEL & RESTAURANT

BROME, EYE, SUFFOLK IP23 8AJ
Tel: 01379 870326 **International:** +44 (0)1379 870326
Web: www.condenastjohansens.com/cornwallis **E-mail:** generalmanager.cornwallis@ohiml.com

Our inspector loved: *The great feeling of peace and relaxation at this beautiful grade 2 listed hotel.*

Price Guide:
single from £95
double from £115

Awards/Recognition: 1 AA Rosette 2011–2012

Location: On A140; Diss, 2-min drive; Ipswich, 30-min drive; Bury St Edmunds, 30-min drive

Attractions: Suffolk Coast; Bury St Edmunds; Bressingham Gardens and Steam Museum

The Cornwallis is reached via a long avenue of mature lime trees. A pretty and romantic dower house dating back to the 16th-century awaits you and tranquil topiary gardens and woodlands surround. The house has clung on to many of its interesting original features; an intriguing script above the stairwell, oak panelling, working fireplaces and in the Tudor bar, serving cask ales, a 30-foot deep well. The oldest areas have low beams and quaint sloping floors, while the later Victorian addition features loftier spaces. All bedrooms are unique. The Lexington Restaurant prides itself on its cuisine, inspired by the excellent local Suffolk produce. Lighter but equally delicious meals can be enjoyed in the 16th-century Tudor bar.

THE OLDE BULL INN

BARTON MILLS, BURY ST EDMUNDS, SUFFOLK IP28 6AA
Tel: 01638 711001 **International:** +44 (0)1638 711001
Web: www.condenastjohansens.com/oldebullinn **E-mail:** bookings@bullinn-bartonmills.com

Our inspector loved: The welcoming bar and restaurant with good traditional fare and comfortable rooms.

Price Guide:
single from £79
double from £89

Awards/Recognition: 1 AA Rosette 2011-2012

Location: Just off A11; Newmarket, 7 miles; Bury St Edmunds, 13 miles; Cambridge, 21.5 miles

Attractions: Thetford Forest - Go Ape and Center Parcs; Newmarket Racecourse; Cambridge Colleges and Punting; Ely Cathedral

This historic hotel - dating back to the 16th century as a coaching inn – was lovingly restored and refurbished by owners Cheryl and Wayne in 2007 to create a little gem. With great respect to its original features, the Inn is now a happy blend of old and new, rambling and picturesque, complete with courtyard, quaint gables and a distinct boutique style. All 14 bedrooms are individually furnished with rich fabrics and wallpapers and are complemented by crisp white bathrooms. Cosy up in your room and enjoy the LCD flat-screen TV, or head to the restaurant and informal Public Bar where a warm welcome awaits. Whether you're dining on AA Rosette-awarded English meals with a twist in The Oak Room Restaurant or enjoying pub-style food in the Public Bar by the roaring fire, you'll also find good wines and real ales on tap to tempt you. The Inn hosts many special events, including live music, all year, and is available for celebrations and private dining.

SATIS HOUSE HOTEL & RESTAURANT

MAIN ROAD, YOXFORD, SAXMUNDHAM, SUFFOLK IP17 3EX
Tel: 01728 668418 **International:** +44 (0)1728 668418
Web: www.condenastjohansens.com/satishouse **E-mail:** enquiries@satishouse.co.uk

Our inspector loved: *The stylish decor and relaxing in the garden with a pre dinner apéritif. The perfect start to a relaxing break.*

Price Guide:
single from £65
double from £95

Awards/Recognition: 2 AA Rosettes 2011-2012; Best Breakfast Award - English Tourist Board 2009-2010; Voted Top 3 Restaurants in Suffolk - EDP Suffolk Magazine 2009

Location: A1120, 1-min drive; A12, 1-min drive, Southwold, 7 miles; Aldeburgh, 12 miles;

Attractions: Southwold; Aldedurgh; Minsmere Nature Reserve; Snape Maltings Concert Hall

Perfect for weekend getaways and special mid week breaks, this exquisite Suffolk hotel is a relaxing, comfortable retreat in a charming setting. Elegant and welcoming, Satis House is a Grade II listed country house tucked away amidst 3 acres of beautiful parkland. Its tasteful interior is a wonderful example of modern design sympathetic to the house's 18th-century origins, evident in the spacious bedrooms that feature fashionable fabrics and prints alongside stylish furnishings and modern fittings. For a romantic stay, why not book a guest room with a luxury four-poster bed. Start the day with a hearty meal consisting of smoked salmon or smoked kippers or enjoy a full Suffolk breakfast accompanied by Earl Grey prunes and local dairy produce. Dinner is equally tempting at the award-winning restaurant where modern British cuisine is created from locally sourced produce wherever possible. Recipient of the English Tourist Board's highly regarded Gold Award.

THE CROWN INN

THE GREEN, PETWORTH ROAD, CHIDDINGFOLD, SURREY GU8 4TX
Tel: 01428 682255 **International:** +44 (0)1428 682255
Web: www.condenastjohansens.com/crownchiddingfold **E-mail:** enquiries@thecrownchiddingfold.com

Our inspector loved: The perfect English setting and romantic atmosphere enjoyed in this centuries old village inn.

Price Guide:
single £100
superior double £125
four-poster from £140
suite £200

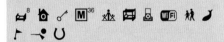

An idyllic English pub and now just one of 10 UK inns to be awarded 5 AA stars, The Crown Inn nestles in a quiet corner of the picture perfect village green of Chiddingfold. Recently refurbished, the Old World charm of the property has been lovingly maintained and sympathetically blended with a more sophisticated and contemporary design. Beautiful stained-glass windows provide a stunning backdrop to the large dining rooms, whilst the downstairs bar has a more informal ambience. There is a passion for food here and excellent seasonal ingredients are used to serve "proper pub food" alongside a superb extensive selection of wines and real ales. The bedrooms have all been renovated; some have stunning ancient beams and gently sloping floors that create a truly romantic and welcoming haven. Within an hour's drive of London there can be few better locations for a weekend break or even just a cracking Sunday lunch in front of a roaring log fire in winter!

Awards/Recognition: Condé Nast Johansens Most Excellent Inn 2010

Location: On the A283; Guildford, 13.5 miles; London Waterloo, 40-min train

Attractions: Petworth House; Ramster Gardens; Lurgashall Winery; Goodwood

THE SWAN INN

PETWORTH ROAD, CHIDDINGFOLD, SURREY GU8 4TY
Tel: 01428 684688 **International:** +44 (0)1428 684688
Web: www.condenastjohansens.com/swansurrey **E-mail:** info@theswaninnchiddingfold.com

Our inspector loved: The great food, stylish décor and unpretentious atmosphere. Well worth a drive out of London and even better if you stay the night! This is a real find.

Price Guide:
double £100
family £150
suite £170

Location: On the A283; Guildord, 13.5 miles; London Waterloo, 40-min train

Attractions: Petworth House & Park; Goodwood Estate; Cowdray Park; Ramster Gardens

Set on the borders of picture perfect West Sussex and Surrey countryside, this small, privately owned inn has the atmosphere of a warm, friendly "local". The added bonus of sumptuous bedrooms luxuriously furnished and offering high quality linens and amenities, means you can fully unwind and make the most of your visit. No expense has been spared in creating a relaxed, comfortable bolthole where you can also enjoy the very best of British food. Whether you're planning a special occasion, corporate lunch or private dining, menus are created from the finest seasonal, local produce: ham hock terrine with homemade piccalilli, chargrilled rib eye steak and a fabulous selection of cheeses and desserts are just a few dishes to tempt you! The same care is taken in sourcing drinks for the bar, with artisan beers and lager on tap, and proper coffee, brewed the Italian way. After a delicious breakfast, explore the glorious countryside, play a round of golf or head to the coast.

The Castle Inn

CASTLE COMBE, WILTSHIRE SN14 7HN
Tel: 01249 783030 **International:** +44 (0)1249 783030
Web: www.condenastjohansens.com/castleinn **E-mail:** enquiries@castle-inn.info

Our inspector loved: The fabulous new bedrooms and bathrooms. The mix of contemporary and traditional styles that complement this beautiful old inn.

Price Guide:
single £70-£165
double £115-£195

Nestled in the heart of the Cotswolds, in the picturesque village of Castle Combe, previously crowned the "Prettiest Village in England", this charming inn can trace its origins back to the 12th century. Architecturally, little has changed in the village since the 15th century; there are no street lights or TV aerials, and The Castle Inn stands proudly in its beautiful market place. An extensive and considerate recent restoration has created a wonderfully contemporary hotel, whilst preserving its unique historic character and many ancient features, perfectly complementing the tranquillity of the village. 11 delightful bedrooms are individually furnished with sumptuous fabrics and offer luxurious bathrooms and every modern comfort. Dining venues include a cosy bar with an open fire, the more intimate Oak Room and the relaxed Terrace Patio, perfect for enjoying a selection of traditional meals and an á la carte menu in the evenings.

Location: M4 jct 17, 5 miles; Bath, 13 miles; Chippenham Railway Station, 6 miles; Bristol Airport, 27 miles

Attractions: Bath; Lacock; Cotswold Villages; Bradford on Avon

The Old Rectory

IPSLEY LANE, IPSLEY, NEAR REDDITCH, WORCESTERSHIRE B98 0AP
Tel: 01527 523000 **International:** +44 (0)1527 523000
Web: www.condenastjohansens.com/oldrecipsley **E-mail:** ipsleyoldrectory@aol.com

Our inspector loved: *Enjoying dinner in the conservatory with its outlook over the beautiful gardens.*

Price Guide:
single from £87
double/twin from £117

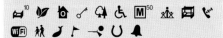

Location: A435, 2 miles; M42 jct 3, 7 miles; Redditch, 3 miles; Birmingham International Airport and Railway Station, 13 miles

Attractions: Stratford-upon-Avon; Warwick Castle; The Cotswolds; Birmingham Bullring; Arrow Valley Country Park

A quintessentially English country house hotel tucked away in the heart of England, The Old Rectory's warmth and personal hospitality makes it a relaxing and comfortable venue for both work and play. Set in 3 acres of wooded gardens, this Elizabethan and Georgian rectory radiates charm and peace, and provides the perfect setting for short breaks, conferences, business meetings and family occasions including weddings. This is truly a hotel for all seasons. The fire in the drawing room welcomes you in the autumn and winter and the scent of flowers in the gardens is irresistible during the spring and summer. Each bedroom is quite different; one is reputedly haunted, others have exposed beams and one has a barrel ceiling. Dinner is served in the conservatory restaurant where menus feature dishes prepared on the premises from the freshest seasonal produce to a backdrop of pretty garden views.

THE WHITE LION HOTEL

HIGH STREET, UPTON-UPON-SEVERN, NEAR MALVERN, WORCESTERSHIRE WR8 0HJ
Tel: 01684 592551 **International:** +44 (0)1684 592551
Web: www.condenastjohansens.com/whitelionupton **E-mail:** info@whitelionhotel.biz

Our inspector loved: Jon and Richard's excellent food and the great traditional hospitality.

Price Guide:
single from £70–£90
double from £99
four-poster from £125

Awards/Recognition: 1 AA Rosette 2011-2012

Location: On the A4104; A38, 1.5 miles; M5 jct 7, 8 miles; Worcester, 11 miles

Attractions: Worcester; Malvern Hills; Ledbury; Tewkesbury Abbey; The Three Counties Show Ground and Upton Jazz Festival

A great walking holiday destination in the Malvern Hills, near Cheltenham, this charming coaching inn is now 500 years old, dating back to the 16th century. Proudly ensuring The White Lion Hotel's superb reputation, owners Jon and Chris Lear celebrate this landmark achievement with special packages throughout the year. Those with a literary mindset will appreciate Henry Fielding's words in "The History of Tom Jones" where the property is described as "the fairest inn on the street" and "a house of exceedingly good repute." Some of its bedrooms trace back to 1510 and also boast literary associations: the Rose Room and Wild Goose Room are also named in a Fielding book. The award-winning Pepperpot Brasserie serves fine dishes with flair and plenty of seasonal influence. As a member of CAMRA supporters for "real ale," the bar is stocked for aficionados, and each summer, the hotel holds its own mini-beer festival!

THE TRADDOCK

AUSTWICK, NORTH YORKSHIRE LA2 8BY
Tel: 015242 51224 **International:** +44 (0)15242 51224
Web: www.condenastjohansens.com/austwick **E-mail:** info@austwicktraddock.co.uk

Our inspector loved: The welcome and hospitality at this award winning, charming family run hotel.

Price Guide:
single £90–£125
double/twin £99–£190

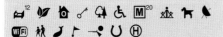

Awards/Recognition: Condé Nast Johansens Award for Innovation in Sustainable Hospitality 2011; Condé Nast Johansens Taittinger Wine List Award, Special Commendation Best Organic Wine List 2010; Condé Nast Johansens Most Excellent Small Hotel of the Year (under 15 rooms) 2009; 2 AA Rosettes 2011-2012

Location: A65, 1 mile; M6 jct 36, 30 miles; Settle, 4 miles; Kirkby Lonsdale, 12 miles

Attractions: Ingleborough Cave; The 3 peaks of Whernside, Pen-y-ghent, Ingleborough; Settle to Carlisle Railway; Yorkshire Dales National Park

Set in 2 acres of peaceful, landscaped gardens in the heart of the Yorkshire Dales National Park is this fine Georgian hotel and restaurant oozing character, charm and the friendliest of hospitality. Enquire about the special breaks available here, a unique location where some of the most sensational limestone scenery in Europe can be found, including several magnificent caves with dazzling stalagmites and stalactites. You can relax after walking and sightseeing tours in the comfortable bar and lounge, warmed in winter by open log fires. Bedrooms are individually designed and beautifully furnished with English antiques. In the restaurant Chef, John Pratt, produces excellent modern, seasonal and local British cuisine,using mostly locally sourced organic produce complemented by an extensive wine list.The winner of Condé Nast Johansens awards for Innovation in Sustainable Hospitality 2011.

DUNSLEY HALL

DUNSLEY, WHITBY, NORTH YORKSHIRE YO21 3TL

Tel: 01947 893437 **International:** +44 (0)1947 893437

Web: www.condenastjohansens.com/dunsleyhall **E-mail:** reception@dunsleyhall.com

Our inspector loved: *This hidden gem with beautifully furnished bedrooms which offer views of the North Yorkshire coast and countryside.*

Price Guide:
single from £95
double/twin from £149
four poster from £180
deluxe from £198

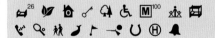

Awards/Recognition: 1 AA Rosette 2011-2012

Location: A171, 2 miles; Whitby, 3 miles; Scarborough, 21 miles

Attractions: Whitby Abbey; Robin Hoods Bay; North Yorkshire Moors Steam Railway; Birthplace of Captain Cook

Dunsley Hall is a super Whitby hotel standing in 4 acres of magnificent landscaped gardens in the North Yorkshire Moors National Park. Virtually unaltered since it was built at the turn of the 20th century, this Victorian house is the perfect base for walking holidays and ideal for wedding receptions that will always be fondly remembered. Some of the individually decorated bedrooms, 2 with four-poster beds, enjoy a fantastic view of the sea, just a few minutes walk away, and feature fine fabrics and furniture. All bedrooms are non-smoking. Mellow oak panelling, a handsome inglenook carved fireplace and stained-glass windows enhance the drawing room's relaxing and restful atmosphere. From the Oak Room, Terrace Suite or Pyman Bar, you can enjoy award-winning regional dishes and seafood specialities made from only the freshest of ingredients. There is also a cottage available by prior request.

HEY GREEN COUNTRY HOUSE HOTEL

WATERS ROAD, MARSDEN, WEST YORKSHIRE HD7 6NG
Tel: 01484 848000 **International:** +44 (0)1484 848000
Web: www.condenastjohansens.com/heygreen **E-mail:** info@heygreen.com

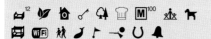

Our inspector loved: *This peaceful retreat overlooking a lake in Last of the Summer Wine country.*

Price Guide:
single from £89
double from £119

Location: A62, 0.33 miles; Marsden, 1 mile; Oldham, 8 miles; Huddersfield, 10 miles

Attractions: Standedge Canal Tunnel; Start of Pennine Way; Last of the Summer Wine Country; Brontë Country

For peace and tranquillity, few places can better this West Yorkshire hotel overlooking the Colne Valley surrounded by green pastures, dry-stone walls and little grey farms tucked into hillsides. A Victorian house with parts dating from the 1700s, the imposing Hey Green stands in 15 acres of grounds encompassing 2 lakes that attract guests to stretch their legs and enjoy water-edge walks among shady trees and knee-high ferns. A warm, welcoming ambience pervades the house where the staff's concern for guest comfort is more typical of a private house rather than a busy hotel. The grand sweeping staircase leads up to the tastefully furnished bedrooms from where you can admire the views of the grounds. Room 11 is worth a special note due to its original 1890s four poster and bathroom with spa bath. The restaurant with its flagstone flooring and open fire is to be found in the oldest part of the building, here the menu emphasises the best of British cuisine.

SCOTLAND

Coleraine
Londonderry
City of Derry
A37
A2
A26
A44
A29
A6
A36
Larne
M2
N14
A5
A505
Belfast
N15
A32
A5
A29
M1
Belfast
A1
A20
N15
A46
A4
A44
A29
A7
N16
Armagh
87
A1
A24
Ballina
Sligo
A28
Newry
N17
N4
N2
Cavan
N3
Dundalk
N26
N5
N5
Longford
M1
Drogheda
Galway
N17
N4
M4
N2
M1
Knock International
Athlone
M7
Dublin
N6
N7
Dublin
Dun Laoghaire
N18
N7
N11
Shannon
Shannon
N24
Kilkenny
Limerick
86
N10
N9
Tralee
N21
N9
N30
Wexford
N20
N24
N9
N25
Killarney
N8
N25
Waterford
N22
Cork
Kenmare
Cork

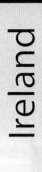

Ireland

For further information on Ireland, please contact:

The Irish Tourist Board
(Bord Fáilte Éireann)
Tel: 0808 234 2009
www.discoverireland.com

Tourism Ireland
Tel: +353 (0)1476 3400
www.tourismireland.com

Irish Georgian Society
74 Merrion Square
Dublin 2
Tel: +353 (0)1676 7053
www.ige.ie

Irish Ferries
Tel: 0818 300400
www.irishferries.com

The Guinness Brewery
Tel: +353 (0)1408 4800
www.guinness-storehouse.com

Aer Lingus
Tel: +353 (0)818 365000
www.aerlingus.com

or see **pages 122-124** for details of local historic houses, castles and gardens to visit during your stay.

For additional places to stay in Ireland, turn to **pages 113-120** where a listing of our Recommended Hotels & Spas can be found.

THE CLIFF TOWN HOUSE

22 ST STEPHEN'S GREEN, DUBLIN
Tel: 00 353 1 638 3939
Web: www.condenastjohansens.com/clifftownhouse **E-mail:** info@theclifftownhouse.com

Our inspector loved: The super location and pure "buzz" of this stylish boutique hotel.

Price Guide: (euro)
single from €125
double from €145

Location: Centre of Dublin

Attractions: St Sephen's Green; National Art Gallery; Trinity College; The Irish Parliament

The Cliff Townhouse is a luxury Georgian hotel situated on St Stephen's Green, a quiet haven in the heart of Dublin's finest shopping precinct. Its classic ambience and boutique style offers 10 comfortable bedrooms that are beautifully designed with thoughtful attention to each detail. As you relax in your room, admire the views over St Stephen's Green, only a stone's throw from the historic centre of Dublin. In fact, just to the side of this charming hotel is the National Art Gallery and Trinity College Dublin, so if you are a culture lover, this hotel is ideal for you. You will not be disappointed by the quality of the food offered here: each meal is meticulously prepared with the best ingredients to create a traditionally Irish meal with a modern twist. Together with excellent service and a great atmosphere, your dinner will be an unforgettable treat.

CASTLE LESLIE

CASTLE LESLIE ESTATE, GLASLOUGH, COUNTY MONAGHAN
Tel: 00 353 47 88100
Web: www.condenastjohansens.com/castleleslie **E-mail:** reservations@castleleslie.com

Our inspector loved: *The fabulous choice of outdoor activities and the warm hospitality.*

Price Guide: (euro)
single €180
double €240
suite €280

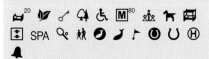

Location: Dublin Airport, 81 miles; Belfast Airport, 53 miles

Attractions: Navan Fort; Patrick Kavanagh Centre; The Planetarium

Castle Leslie is one of the last great Irish estates still owned by its founding family. Just 80 minutes from Dublin and 1 hour from Belfast, it enjoys a peaceful setting within a 1,000-acre estate dotted with ancient forests and lakes. Offering warm Irish hospitality and complete escapism, the castle's rich history is evident throughout. From traditional breakfasts to formal afternoon tea and candle-lit dinners, guests savour the finest Irish cuisine with many dishes cleverly reinvented from the Castle Leslie Estate Cook Book of centuries-old family recipes. Spend time exploring the picturesque Estate on foot or on horseback, or go fishing on one of Ireland's best pike lakes. Alternatively, escape to the cosy private cinema for an afternoon. For pure relaxation, the Victorian Treatment Rooms await, with outdoor hot tubs and authentic Victorian steam boxes to soothe tired muscles.

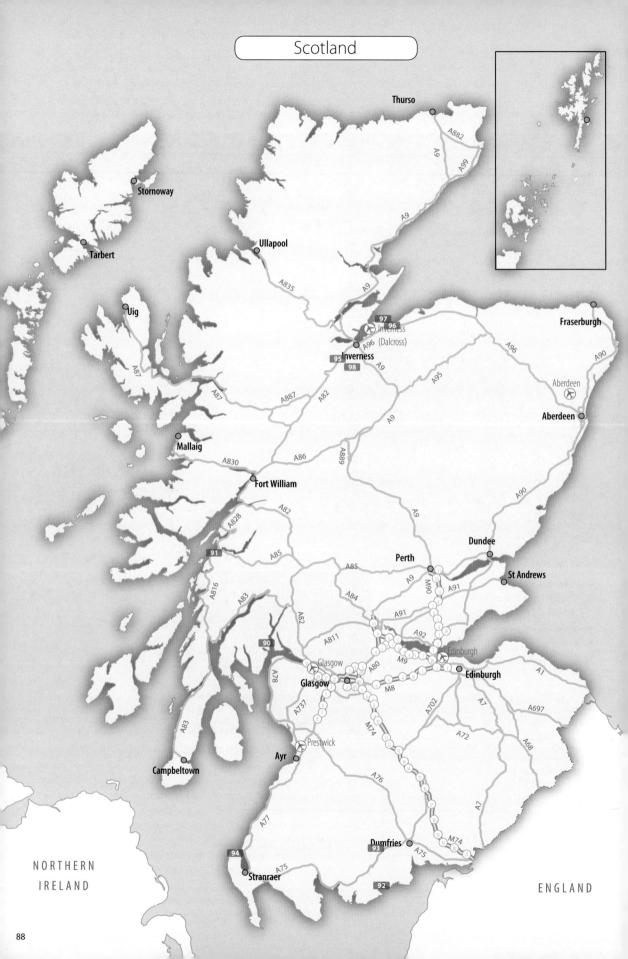

Scotland

Thurso

A882

A9

A99

Stornoway

Tarbert

Ullapool

A835

A9

Uig

97
96
Inverness
(Dalcross)

A96

Fraserburgh

A96

A90

A87

95 Inverness
98

A9

A887

A82

A95

Aberdeen

Mallaig

A830

A86

A889

Aberdeen

Fort William

A82

A90

91

A828

A85

A816

A83

A82

A811

A85

A84

A91

Perth

A9

Dundee

St Andrews

A91

90

A78

Glasgow

A80

A91

A92

Edinburgh

Glasgow

M9

Edinburgh

A1

A737

M8

A702

A7

A697

Prestwick

M74

A72

A68

Ayr

A76

A7

Campbeltown

A77

M74

93 Dumfries

A75

94

A75

92

Stranraer

NORTHERN

IRELAND

ENGLAND

88

Scotland

For further information on Scotland, please contact:

Visit Scotland
Ocean Point 1,
94 Ocean Drive
Edinburgh EH6 6JH
Tel: 0845 22 55 121
www.visitscotland.com

Greater Glasgow & Clyde Valley Tourist Board
11 George Square
Glasgow G2 1DY
Tel: +44 (0)141 566 0800
www.seeglasgow.com

Edinburgh & Lothians Tourist Board
Tel: 0845 2255 121
www.edinburgh.org

Visit Scottish Borders
Tel: 0845 2255 121
www.scot-borders.co.uk

Loganair
Tel: +44 (0)141 8487594
www.loganair.co.uk

Flybe
Tel: 0871 200 2000
www.flybe.com

or see **pages 122-124** for details of local historic houses, castles and gardens to visit during your stay.

For additional places to stay in Scotland, turn to **pages 113-120** where a listing of our Recommended Hotels & Spas Guide can be found.

The Majestic Line - Argyll Coast Cruises

3 MELVILLE CRESCENT, EDINBURGH EH3 7HW
Tel: 0131 623 5012 **International:** +44 (0)131 623 5012
Web: www.condenastjohansens.com/themajesticline **E-mail:** info@themajesticline.co.uk

Our inspector loved: *The culinary delights on this exceptionally comfortable boat with the ever-changing scenery.*

Price Guide: (all inclusive)
£965 per person (3-nights)
£1830 per person (6-nights)
2 cabins per cruise reserved for single passengers (no single supplement)

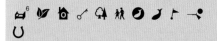

Location: Holy Loch: A815; M8, 30-min; Dunoon, 5-min; Glasgow Airport, 1-hour. Oban: A85, M, 2-hour, Glasgow Airport 150-min

Attractions: From Holy Loch: Mount Stuart House; Inveraray Castle; Arran Distillery; Kyles of Bute; Brodick Castle. From Oban: Duart Castle; Tobermory; Fingal's Cave, Staffa; Iona Abbey

Cruise the west coast of Scotland in style, exploring the Inner Hebrides and sheltered sea lochs and islands of Argyll with The Majestic Line. These beautifully converted traditional wooden vessels leave from Oban and Holy Loch to visit idyllic anchorages and historic stopovers whilst offering exceptional hospitality with a menu of local speciality produce, freshly prepared by an onboard chef. With the ability to accommodate 11 guests in 6 en-suite cabins, each charming vessel cruises through breathtaking Highland scenery rich in wildlife and schedules daily shore trips to discover the local heritage. Join a "floating house party" with fellow guests or gather friends and family for a Whole Boat Charter at discounted rates. The Scottish Highlands are nearer than you think: pickups can be arranged from Glasgow Airport for the 1-hour transfer to Holy Loch departures. Transfers to Oban departures can be arranged at a cost.

The Manor House Hotel

GALLANACH ROAD, OBAN, ARGYLL & BUTE PA34 4LS
Tel: 01631 562087 **International:** +44 (0)1631 562087
Web: www.condenastjohansens.com/manorhouseoban **E-mail:** info@manorhouseoban.com

Our inspector loved: *The wonderful cuisine served in the beautiful dining room.*

Price Guide:
single £100-£163
double £153-£228

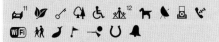

Awards/Recognition: 1 AA Rosette 2011-2012; EatScotland Award 2011

Location: Oban Railway Station, 10-min walk; Glasgow Airport, 150-min drive

Attractions: Ferries to Islands; Sea Life Centre; Bridge over Atlantic and Easdale; Loch Awe

Originally built as a dower house for the Duke of Argyll in the 18th century, this handsome stone built Georgian house resides on the south side of Oban Harbour. Today it is a luxury boutique hotel with an emphasis on fine dining. Head chef, Shaun Squire, creates unique menus each day that focus on the abundance of fresh local seafood, meat and produce. They offer a 5-course prix fixe menu or à la carte dishes such as tian of haggis, Hebridean lobster thermidore and fillet steak with Stornaway black pudding. The 11 distinctive bedrooms are intimate, and some have views across the Bay to Lismore, the Morvern Peninsula and Mull, while others overlook the front garden. Several hiking routes lead from the hotel and there are endless opportunities for days out. You can enjoy ferry trips to discover the wildlife of Mull, visits to Rannoch Moor and Glencoe or guided tours of the Oban Distillery.

BALCARY BAY HOTEL

AUCHENCAIRN, CASTLE DOUGLAS, DUMFRIES & GALLOWAY DG7 1QZ
Tel: 01556 640217/640311 **International:** +44 (0)1556 640217/640311
Web: www.condenastjohansens.com/balcarybay **E-mail:** reservations@balcary-bay-hotel.co.uk

Our inspector loved: *The newly refurbished sea view bedroom is an absolute delight.*

Price Guide: (per person)
single £78
double/twin £70-£85

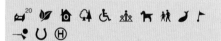

Awards/Recognition: 2 AA Rosettes 2011-2012

Location: Off the A711, 0.9 miles; Auchencairn, 2 miles; Castle Douglas, 9 miles

Attractions: Various Golf Courses; Galloway Wildlife Conservation Park; Threave Castle; Threave Estate and Gardens

At the end of a narrow lane, and enjoying a surprisingly warm Gulf Stream climate, this traditional, secluded hideaway on the Solway Firth is still close to the bustling market towns of Castle Douglas and Dumfries. You will have the reassuring intimacy of a family run hotel, whilst enjoying all the ingredients for a peaceful, romantic visit. As you sit in the lounge overlooking the bay, only the call of sea birds and gently lapping waves compete for your attention. You should make the most of local delicacies such as lobster, prawns and salmon, and the great coastal walks that this corner of Scotland has to offer. Nearby are several excellent golf courses, salmon rivers and trout lochs, sailing, shooting, riding and bird-watching.

CRAIGADAM

KIRKPATRICK DURHAM, KIRKCUDBRIGHTSHIRE DG7 3HU
Tel: 01556 650233 **International:** +44 (0)1556 650233
Web: www.condenastjohansens.com/craigadam **E-mail:** inquiry@craigadam.com

Our inspector loved: Being part of the family in this large comfy country house.

Price Guide:
single from £67
double from £94

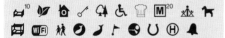

Location: A75, 2 miles; M74, 28 miles; Glasgow Airport, 66 miles

Attractions: Henry Moore, Rodin and Epstein statues on the hills behind the hotel; Drumlandrig Castle; Threave Gardens; The artist's town of Kirkcudbright

It is simply wonderful to soak up the atmosphere of this picturesque country house, nestling in its own estate grounds surrounded by rolling farmland, in Kirkpatrick Durham, close to Galloway National Park. The location and tranquillity of its setting is idyllic for that special occasion or wedding, and the warm friendliness of your hosts makes it feel like a home away from home. The award-winning restaurant has an excellent reputation for delicious home-cooked cuisine, and the lamb and game is sourced from the estate. Craigadam is especially well-known for its rod and gun sporting holidays; there are 25,000 acres of farmland, moorland and woodland on which to stalk! Play a game of billiards or read a book in the cosy drawing room, which has fine views over the Galloway Hills.

CORSEWALL LIGHTHOUSE HOTEL

CORSEWALL POINT, NEAR KIRKCOLM, STRANRAER, DG9 0QG
Tel: 01776 853220 **International:** +44 (0)1776 853220
Web: www.condenastjohansens.com/lighthousehotel **E-mail:** info@lighthousehotel.co.uk

Our inspector loved: After a superb dinner watching the amazing sunset over the Mull of Kintyre with a fine malt in hand.

Price Guide: (including dinner)
single from £85
double £180–£210
suite £210–£290

Awards/Recognition: 1 AA Rosette 2011-2012

Location: A718, 4 miles; Stranraer Ferry, 11 miles; Prestwick Airport, 60 miles

Attractions: Mull of Galloway Lighthouse; Culzean Castle; Logan Botanic Gardens; Day trip to Ireland

Perched high on a clifftop, overlooking the Kintyre peninsula, just yards from a glazier like face, Corsewall Lighthouse is either being dashed by high rising storm spray or smoothed by calmer summer waters at its rocky foot. This sparkling white lighthouse hotel is a gorgeous little retreat that exudes the warmth, charm and romance of its early 19th-century origins with the comforts and style of a very unique hotel. It's a delightfully restored A listed national treasure that you will adore. Views are dazzling by day and star-scattered by night, taking in meadowland and a spectacular seascape brightened by several other working Scottish and Irish lighthouses whose knife-like beams warn of inshore dangers. Flexible accommodation includes three 2-bedroom suites, and the restaurant menu is inspired by seasonal offerings from both the sea and land.

LOCH NESS LODGE

BRACHLA, LOCH NESS-SIDE, INVERNESS IV3 8LA
Tel: 01456 459469 **International:** +44 (0)1456 459469
Web: www.condenastjohansens.com/lochnesslodge **E-mail:** escape@loch-ness-lodge.com

Our inspector loved: *The exquisite food served by such friendly staff in an amazing location.*

Price Guide:
single £195-£355
double £254-£419
cottage from £545 (minimum 3 nights stay)

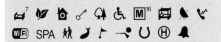

Awards/Recognition: 2 AA Rosettes 2011-2012

Location: Inverness, 15-min drive; Inverness Airport, 40-min drive; Cairngorm National Park, 50-min drive, Isle of Skye, 2 hours drive

Attractions: Cruise on Loch Ness to Urquhart Castle; Culloden Battlefield; Whisky Trail; Cawdor Castle; Rothiemurchus Estate; Eilean Donan Castle

The mix of traditional Scottish architecture and contemporary design works beautifully at Loch Ness Lodge. Its superbly designed bedrooms embody sophisticated style due to their goose down duvets, elegant fabrics and carefully chosen furnishings in natural hues and tones. Each is named after a Highland loch or glen and offers wonderful views. The Lodge is very passionate about the food it serves, and works closely with local artisan suppliers who share their "field to mouth" ethic. The icing on the cake is Escape, the Lodge's spa and therapy suite. Awarded the AA Guest Accommodation of the Year for Scotland 2009/2010, this is the perfect location for an overnight escape or to hire exclusively for a house party, intimate wedding or corporate event. With views over the iconic Loch Ness, the Lodge cannot fail to impress in the location stakes, and does its utmost to ensure you have the perfect Highland experience on every level.

CLUBHOUSE HOTEL

45 SEABANK ROAD, NAIRN, INVERNESS-SHIRE IV12 4EY
Tel: 01667 453321 **International:** +44 (0)1667 453321
Web: www.condenastjohansens.com/clubhousenairn **E-mail:** frontdesk@clubhousehotels.co.uk

Our inspector loved: The stunning traditional exterior stonework that belies an amazingly chic, contemporary interior.

Price Guide:
single £72-£100
double £96-£150

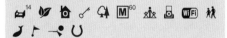

The Moray coast, with its dry, mild climate, firm sand beaches and rocky headlands, has been described as the Scottish Riviera. At its western end in a quiet street, close to the beach and between 2 championship golf courses, is the charming Clubhouse Hotel. Ideal for relaxing family breaks, a romantic weekend or intimate business conference, this former Victorian family villa boasts stunning exterior stonework and a contemporary-styled interior. The bright colour scheme and design is vibrant yet relaxing and reflects the hotel's heritage and formal garden. Bedrooms range from twins to king-size doubles and family rooms to suites. Each is individually styled and offers total comfort and every modern convenience. Before enjoying the home-made Scottish cuisine in the newly refurbished restaurant or more casual Lounge Bar, savour a pre-dinner drink in the cosy Sun Lounge overlooking the garden.

Location: Nairn Railway Station, 20-min walk; Inverness Airport, 6 miles

Attractions: 3 Championship Golf Courses; Loch Ness; Speyside Whisky Trail; Moray Firth Dolphins

INVERAN LODGE

SEAFIELD STREET, NAIRN, INVERNESS-SHIRE IV12 4HG
Tel: 01667 455 666 **International:** +44 (0)1667 455 666
Web: www.condenastjohansens.com/inveranlodge **E-mail:** info@inveranlodge.co.uk

Our inspector loved: The hospitality here never disappoints.

Price Guide:
single from £95
double from £190

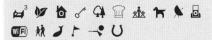

Location: Inverness Airport, 6 miles; Nairn Railway station, 15-min walk

Attractions: 3 championship Golf Courses, on the doorstep; Castle Stuart; Loch Ness; Whisky Trail of Speyside;

Owner, Rosemary Young, provides comfortable and friendly service at her bed and breakfast accommodation that is a home away from home. Situated in a quiet residential area of Nairn, Inveran's tastefully decorated bedrooms have little luxury touches. The elegant dining room offers superb full Scottish breakfasts to help kick-start a day that could have you sampling the town's beautiful beaches, exploring countryside castles, or taking on the challenge of 2 local Championship links golf courses. One of these will host the Curtis Cup in 2012. After a day in the silky Scottish air you can watch spectacular summer sunsets, with a glass of sherry, on the hotel's patio. If you are not heading out for dinner close by, then enjoy one of Rosemary's specially ordered 3-course "Pot Luck Suppers", that may include Scotch broth, Highland beef casserole and raspberry cranachan. At the end of the day retreat to the deep, soft sofas and chairs of the oh-so-peaceful Drawing Room.

THE STEADINGS AT THE GROUSE & TROUT

FLICHITY BY FARR, SOUTH LOCH NESS, INVERNESS IV2 6XD
Tel: 01808 521314 **International:** +44 (0)1808 521314
Web: www.condenastjohansens.com/steadings **E-mail:** stay@steadingshotel.co.uk

Our inspector loved: *Viewing the rare wildlife in the grounds from the comfort of the cosy lounge with dram in hand.*

Price Guide:
single from £82
double £99-£165

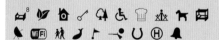

The wonderful panoramic scenery and wildlife to be seen from the conservatory of this rustic, unpretentious Scottish inn is second to none. Built in 1860, The Steadings at The Grouse and Trout originated as outbuildings, thankfully salvaged from the Flichity Inn, destroyed in 1964. Make the most of your break to Scotland: jump on the whisky trail and explore the castles, lochs and glens of the hidden Scottish Highlands, while looking out for herds of deer, wild goats, grouse, and heron landing on the Flichity Loch - if you're really lucky you might even spot an osprey whisking away a salmon, or a stoat playing with the resident hare family on the hotel's lawn. Enjoy a local beer in The Grouse & Trout Lounge Bar and delicious Scottish and international food alongside an excellent wine list and, of course, fine Scottish malt whiskies. A deserved finalist in the Condé Nast Johansens Readers Award 2009.

Location: On the B851 ; A9 to Fort Augustus Road, 7 miles; Inverness, 12 miles; Inverness Airport, 20 miles

Attractions: Loch Ruthved Nature Reserve; Cawdor Castle; Loch Ness and Caledonian Canal; Culloden Battlefield; Cairngorm Mountains

Wales

Holyhead

A55

A55

103 Llandudno

A55

A5

Caernarfon

A470

Wrexham

A483

A534

107

A5

A494

A487

Snowdonia
National Park

A5

A494

A5

65

A470

A470

106 Dolgellau

105

A458

A487

A470

A483

Aberystwyth

A470

A44

A470

A483

ENGLAND

A487

A44

A470

A44

A483

102

A487

A483

A470

A44

Fishguard

A483

A470

A438

A40

Brecon

A470

A40

A479

108

Carmarthen

A40

A483

A470

A40

110

A40

A477

A48

Brecon Beacons National Park

Abergavenny

A40

Pembroke

A483

A465

A449

Swansea

M4

109

M4

A470

Cardiff

Cardiff

Wales

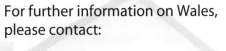

For further information on Wales, please contact:

Wales Tourist Board
Tel: 0845 010 3300
www.visitwales.com

North Wales Tourism
Tel: 0845 450 5885
www.nwt.co.uk

Mid Wales Tourism
E-mail: info@midwalestourism.co.uk
www.visitmidwales.co.uk

South West Wales Tourism Partnership
Tel: +44 (0)1558 669091
www.swwtp.co.uk

Cadw: Welsh Historic Monuments
Tel: +44 (0)1443 33 6000
E-mail: cadw@wales.gsi.gov.uk
www.cadw.wales.gov.uk

Millennium Stadium
Tel: 08442 777 888
www.millenniumstadium.com

or see **pages 122-124** for details of local historic houses, castles and gardens to visit during your stay.

For additional places to stay in the Wales, turn to **pages 113-120** where a listing of our Recommended Hotels & Spa Guide can be found.

Plas Dinas Country House, Gwynedd, Wales – p107

PENBONTBREN

GLYNARTHEN, NEAR CARDIGAN, LLANDYSUL, CEREDIGION SA44 6PE
Tel: 01239 810248 **International:** +44 (0)1239 810248
Web: www.condenastjohansens.com/penbontbren **E-mail:** contact@penbontbren.com

Our inspector loved: The luxurious suites that open out to private patios with views over the gardens and countryside.

Price Guide:
single from £70
double £95-110

Effortlessly charming, this luxury bed and breakfast has been lovingly converted from a traditional Welsh farm into beautiful double suites and a self-catering cottage. Nestled in 32 acres of grounds it has views across the idyllic countryside to the Preseli Mountains and is just 2 miles from sandy beaches owned by The National Trust. Each suite is full of character located in the former stable, mill, threshing barn or granary. Furnished to an impeccable standard, with spacious sitting rooms, private gardens and king-size beds, careful attention to detail includes sumptuous bedding and The White Company toiletries. Enjoy breakfast in the breakfast room or indulge yourself with breakfast in bed. Fresh, wholesome ingredients are locally sourced and provide the perfect start to the day. Penbontbren holds an alcohol licence and each suite has a well stocked mini-bar. In addition, an award-winning farm shop is on the doorstep. Just watch out for the free running chickens!

Location: A487, 1 miles; Cardigan, 7 miles; Carmarthen, 25 miles; Aberystwyth, 28 miles

Attractions: Cardigan Bay; Welsh Coast & National Trust Beaches; National Botanical Gardens of Wales; Llanerchaeron (NT)

SYCHNANT PASS COUNTRY HOUSE

SYCHNANT PASS ROAD, CONWY LL32 8BJ

Tel: 01492 596868 **International:** +44 (0)1492 596868

Web: www.condenastjohansens.com/sychnantpass **E-mail:** info@sychnantpasscountryhouse.co.uk

Our inspector loved: *The picturesque and peaceful location on the edge of Snowdonia National Park.*

Price Guide:
single £70-£140
double/twin £95-£170
suite £125-£195

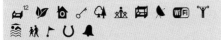

Location: A55, 2 miles; Conwy, 1.5 miles; Chester, 46 miles; Holyhead Port for Ireland, 38 miles

Attractions: Snowdonia; Conwy Castle; Bodnant Garden

Enveloped by the natural beauty of Snowdonia National Park, Sychnant Pass Country House is an elegant, charming hotel. Surrounded by 3 acres of landscaped gardens, unfenced roads, wandering sheep and roaming wild ponies, it is difficult not to feel relaxed and invigorated within this magnificent, remote environment. The bedrooms are beautifully decorated, each to its own high specifications with an individual character. Four of the suites have sitting rooms and some have galleries and terraces looking out to the stunning views towards the medieval walled town of Conwy. Be sure to take a dip in the heated indoor pool, which was imported from South Africa, or simply relax on a sunbed beside the pool or on the terrace with a glass of wine. In the evening, savour a romantic dinner by candlelight in the restaurant whose daily changing menu uses fresh, locally sourced ingredients whenever possible.

PORTH TOCYN COUNTRY HOUSE HOTEL

ABERSOCH, PWLLHELI, GWYNEDD LL53 7BU

Tel: 01758 713303 **International:** +44 (0)1758 713303

Web: www.condenastjohansens.com/porthtocyn **E-mail:** bookings@porthtocyn.fsnet.co.uk

Our inspector loved: *This delightfully friendly and relaxing hideaway hotel, a perfect place for a seaside stay.*

Price Guide: (including continental breakfast)
single £70–£90
double/twin £99–£180

From the moment you walk into Porth Tocyn Country House Hotel you will feel relaxed, comfortable and at home which is why so many guests return again and again. Intimate sitting rooms overflow with country antiques and the softest of enveloping armchairs. The lawned gardens extend towards Cardigan Bay and the mountains of Snowdonia, plus you are close to the glorious beaches of Abersoch and the Llyn Peninsula. Superbly located for some of the best walking and golf in North Wales, this delightful hotel has been owned by one family for 3 generations. Most bedrooms have seaviews and some are ideal for families For that extra sense of privacy there is a gorgeous 2-bedroom self-contained cottage within the grounds. Memorable dinners are served in the 2 Rosette award-winning restaurant and summer lunches can be taken on the terrace or poolside. Closed November to March.

Awards/Recognition: Condé Nast Johansens Most Excellent Value Award 2008; 2 AA Rosettes 2011-2012

Location: A499, 3 miles; A479, 9 miles; Chester, 100 miles; Shrewsbury, 104 miles

Attractions: Snowdonia National Park; Portmeirion; Lloyd George Museum; Heritage Coast Line

BAE ABERMAW

PANORAMA HILL, BARMOUTH, GWYNEDD LL42 1DQ
Tel: 01341 280550 **International:** +44 (0)1341 280550
Web: www.condenastjohansens.com/baeabermaw **E-mail:** enquiries@baeabermaw.com

Our inspector loved: *The chic and contemporary feel of this seaside property overlooking Barmouth Estuary, harbour and beach, and the delicious free-range eggs from the resident hens in the gardens.*

Price Guide:
single £75–£99
double/twin £98–£145

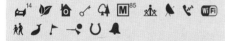

Awards/Recognition: 1 AA Rosette 2011-2012

Location: A496, 0.25 miles; A470, 8 miles; Birmingham Airport, 108 miles; Manchester Airport, 110 miles

Attractions: Mawddach Estuary; Snowdonia National Park; Royal St Davids Golf Course; Portmeirion

This small hotel built from natural stone and overlooking the lovely Mawddach Estuary, is backed by Snowdonia National Park. Owners David and Suzi Reeve have created a truly impressive retreat offering the best of everything, setting itself above the label of "seaside hotel". Cool neutral colours - white, cream, flax, beige - stripped floorboards and streamlined sofas suggest a minimalist feel, whilst natural stone and wood is prominent in the excellent restaurant. The cuisine has some modern and exciting interpretations of classic British dishes with a French influence. Local produce is much in use, particularly Welsh black beef, marsh lamb and sole, plus a choice of vegetarian options. The hotel also serves Sunday lunch and classic afternoon teas. Bedrooms are stylishly decorated and feature deep baths and luxurious toiletries.

LLWYNDU FARMHOUSE

LLANABER, NR BARMOUTH, GWYNEDD LL42 1RR
Tel: 01341 280144 **International:** +44 (0)1341 280144
Web: www.condenastjohansens.com/llwyndu **E-mail:** intouch@llwyndu-farmhouse.co.uk

Our inspector loved: This charming cosy farmhouse with stunning panoramic views of long sandy beaches and the sea.

Price Guide:
single from £75
double £98–£125

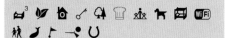

If searching for a small hotel that is both historic and unspoilt, then this is the perfect place to stay. Overlooking Cardigan Bay, this grade 2 listed farmhouse has been lovingly restored by owners Peter and Paula Thompson. Full of character and charm, many quirky original features have been kept including the inglenook fireplaces, stone staircase and even a sink fitted onto a door. Two of the three bedrooms have four posters and whilst all have up to date comforts they exude the personality of a welcoming 16th century home. In the evenings you can dine by candle light in the cosy and warm restaurant, perfect for an intimate evening or gathering of friends. Dishes are imaginatively prepared by Peter who uses fresh Welsh ingredients with flair. You shouldn't leave without trying a national favourite - Welsh rarebit with laver bread. Recipient of an AA dinner award.

Location: A 496, 0.25 miles; Barmouth, 2 miles; A 470, 12 miles; A487, 14 miles

Attractions: Harlech Castle; Little Railways of Wales; Portmeirion; Snowdonia National Park

PLAS DINAS COUNTRY HOUSE

BONTNEWYDD, CAERNARFON, GWYNEDD LL54 7YF
Tel: 01286 830214   **International:** +44 (0)1286 830214
Web: www.condenastjohansens.com/plasdinas   **E-mail:** info@plasdinas.co.uk

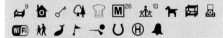

Our inspector loved: *The unique family history of this charming country house.*

Price Guide:
single from £110
double £140-£250

Location: A487, 500yds; Caernarfon, 2 miles; Bangor, 15-min drive; Chester, 1-hour drive

Attractions: Snowdon; Caernafon Castle; Portmeirion; Welsh Highland Railway

Surrounded by 15 acres of grounds, the Grade II listed Plas Dinas is a charming, whitewashed country home ideal for family get togethers, exclusive hire, romantic honeymoons and stress-free breaks. With an interesting history featuring royal connections, this was the country retreat of the Armstrong-Jones family, whose latter day son became the first Earl of Snowdon following marriage to the Queen's sister, Princess Margaret. She spent happy days here and a stunning, super deluxe suite is named after her with a magnificent antique four-poster bed, roll-top bath for two and views towards Snowdonia. The whole house is striking with beautiful furnishings, comfy sofas and chairs, gilt framed portraits and 5-star dining. This is a great base for exploring the area as well as Caernarfon, the ceremonial capital of Wales whose 13th-century castle saw the birth of the first Prince of Wales in 1284 and the investiture of Prince Charles to the title in 1969.

THE BELL AT SKENFRITH

SKENFRITH, MONMOUTHSHIRE NP7 8UH
Tel: 01600 750235 **International:** +44 (0)1600 750235
Web: www.condenastjohansens.com/bellskenfrith **E-mail:** enquiries@skenfrith.co.uk

Our inspector loved: The comfortable restaurant and bar serving superb cuisine plus the well appointed bedrooms.

Price Guide:
single £75–£120 (not available at weekends)
double/twin £110–£170
four-poster £195–£220

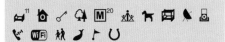

This beautifully restored old coaching inn dates back to the 17th century and is surrounded by unspoiled Monmouthshire countryside overlooking historic Norman castle ruins. It's a dream come true if you're looking for a quiet retreat to escape to, with its roaring log fires, flagstone floors, stunning oak beams and comfy sofas. Bedrooms are homely with traditional Welsh blankets, the finest linen and views of the Welsh hills or River Monnow. In the evenings sip a glass of wine or real ale before tucking into canapés followed by a delicious dinner. Created by the award-winning kitchen, much of the food is grown in The Bell's own organic kitchen garden or by trusted local suppliers.

Awards/Recognition: Condé Nast Johansens/ Champagne Taittinger Special Commendation Champagne List 2011; 2 AA Rosettes 2011-2012

Location: Off the B4521; A466, 3.4 miles; A49, 7.2 miles; Monmouth, 8 miles

Attractions: Llanthony Priory, Abergavenny; Tintern Abbey; Monmouth; Ross-on-Wye

Newbridge On Usk

TREDUNNOCK, NEAR USK, MONMOUTHSHIRE NP15 1LY
Tel: 01633 451000 **International:** +44 (0)1633 451000
Web: www.condenastjohansens.com/newbridgeonusk **E-mail:** NewbridgeOnUsk@celtic-manor.com

Our inspector loved: *The picture-perfect setting, intimate restaurant and bar and stylish lodge-style bedrooms.*

Price Guide: (full, non-refundable pre-payment required at time of booking)
single from £59
double from £70

Awards/Recognition: 1 AA Rosette 2011-2012

Location: Usk, 5 miles; Caerleon, 4.5 miles; Monmouth, 21 miles; Cardiff, 22 miles

Attractions: Tintern Abbey; Raglan Castle; Cardiff Castle; Caerleon Roman Museum

Part of Celtic Manor Resort, this award-winning AA Rosette Restaurant with Rooms is a charming 200-year-old inn idyllically set on the banks of the river Usk. Within the pretty village of Tredunnock, this welcoming country inn is a convenient short drive from the Severn Crossing and Cardiff yet feels miles off the beaten track. Wooden flooring, traditional beamed ceilings, cosy nooks and open fires set the inviting scene, and tastefully styled guest rooms offer sheer comfort. Each bedroom has its own individual character, designed with oak and teak furnishings complete with bathrooms decorated in limestone and marble tiles with oak handmade fittings. Next door is the impressive gastro-pub where wholesome country dishes are passionately created from fresh locally sourced produce. However, guests at the inn may patronize the variety of dining options available in the Resort. Furthermore, guests are entitled to complimentary use of all the Resort's five-star facilities.

The Crown At Whitebrook

WHITEBROOK, MONMOUTHSHIRE NP25 4TX
Tel: 01600 860254 **International:** +44 (0)1600 860254
Web: www.condenastjohansens.com/crownatwhitebrook **E-mail:** info@crownatwhitebrook.co.uk

Our inspector loved: The first class food and service offered in a picturesque village setting.

Price Guide:
single £90
double £100–£120

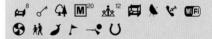

Awards/Recognition: 1 Star Michelin 2011; 2 AA Rosettes 2011-2012; 7/10 The Which Good Food Guide

Location: A466, 2 miles; B4293, 3 miles; Monmouth, 5 miles

Attractions: Monmouth; Wye Valley; Tintern Abbey; Chepstow Racecourse

Visitors to The Crown At Whitebrook come away waxing lyrical about its romantic, tranquil setting, great rooms and fabulous food; and we would have to agree! Dubbed Wales' first restaurant with rooms this is a haven for food lovers and with its growing reputation, Head Chef James Sommerin ensures the food takes centre stage with his modern Michelin Star menus bursting with classic French style. You won't feel overawed in the restaurant here however, as the atmosphere is unpretentious and intimate, with friendly, attentive service. All 8 bedrooms have been lovingly refurbished and look across rolling countryside. Impressive facilities such as flat-screen TVs, Internet and "comfort cool" heating systems are the icing on the cake. Outside the surrounding designated area of outstanding natural beauty is bound to entice you to explore. Wake up each morning to a sumptuous Welsh breakfast!

L'OCCITANE
EN PROVENCE

A true story

The scents and traditions of the land of Provence lie at the heart of L'OCCITANE. It has gained its most precious secrets from this unique region, where Nature is so beautiful and flowers have long yielded their benefits.

From their harvests come natural and authentic skincare products, fragrances and toiletries, effective and deliciously tempting.

www.loccitane.com

Experience L'OCCITANE amenities in the best properties around the world.
L'OCCITANE is proud to be a Condé Nast Johansens Preferred Partner.

Hotels - Great Britain & Ireland

Properties listed below can be found in our Recommended Hotels & Spas – Great Britain & Ireland 2012 Guide

CHANNEL ISLANDS - JERSEY (ST BRELADE)

The Atlantic Hotel

Le Mont de la Pulente, St Brelade, Jersey, JE3 8HE

Tel: 01534 744101
www.condenastjohansens.com/atlantic

CHANNEL ISLANDS - JERSEY (ST HELIER)

The Club Hotel & Spa, Bohemia Restaurant

Green Street, St Helier, Jersey JE2 4UH

Tel: 01534 876500
www.condenastjohansens.com/theclubjersey

CHANNEL ISLANDS - JERSEY (ST SAVIOUR)

Longueville Manor

St Saviour, Jersey, Channel Islands JE2 7WF

Tel: 01534 725501
www.condenastjohansens.com/longuevillemanor

BATH & NORTH EAST SOMERSET - BATH

Dukes Hotel

Great Pulteney Street, Bath, Somerset BA2 4DN

Tel: 01225 787960
www.condenastjohansens.com/dukesbath

BEDFORDSHIRE - LUTON

Luton Hoo Hotel, Golf & Spa

The Mansion House, Luton Hoo, Luton,
Bedfordshire LU1 3TQ

Tel: 01582 734437
www.condenastjohansens.com/lutonhoo

BEDFORDSHIRE - MILTON KEYNES (WOBURN)

Moore Place Hotel

Aspley Guise village, Milton Keynes,
Bedfordshire MK17 8DW

Tel: 01908 282000
www.condenastjohansens.com/mooreplace

BERKSHIRE - ASCOT

Coworth Park

Blacknest Road, Ascot, Berkshire SL5 7SE

Tel: 01344 876600
www.condenastjohansens.com/coworthpark

BERKSHIRE - READING (SONNING-ON-THAMES)

The French Horn

Sonning-on-thames, Berkshire RG4 6TN

Tel: 01189 692204
www.condenastjohansens.com/frenchhorn

BUCKINGHAMSHIRE - MARLOW-ON-THAMES

Danesfield House Hotel and Spa

Henley Road, Marlow-on-Thames,
Buckinghamshire SL7 2EY

Tel: 01628 891010
www.condenastjohansens.com/danesfieldhouse

BUCKINGHAMSHIRE - STOKE POGES (HEATHROW)

Stoke Park

Park Road, Stoke Poges, Buckinghamshire SL2 4PG

Tel: 01753 717171
www.condenastjohansens.com/stokepark

CHESHIRE - KNUTSFORD

The Mere Golf Resort & Spa

Chester Road, Mere, Knutsford, Cheshire WA16 6LJ

Tel: 01565 830155
www.condenastjohansens.com/themereresort

CORNWALL - CARLYON BAY

Carlyon Bay Hotel, Spa & Golf Resort

Sea Road, St Austell, Cornwall PL25 3RD

Tel: 01726 812304
www.condenastjohansens.com/carlyonbay

CORNWALL - CARNE BEACH (NEAR ST MAWES)

The Nare Hotel

Carne Beach, Veryan-in-roseland, Truro,
Cornwall TR2 5PF

Tel: 01872 501111
www.condenastjohansens.com/nare

CORNWALL - FALMOUTH (GYLLYNGVASE BEACH)

St Michael's Hotel & Spa

Gyllyngvase Beach, Falmouth, Cornwall TR11 4NB

Tel: 01326 312707
www.condenastjohansens.com/stmichaelsfalmouth

CORNWALL - FALMOUTH (MAWNAN SMITH)

Budock Vean - The Hotel on the River

Near Helford Passage, Mawnan Smith, Falmouth,
Cornwall TR11 5LG

Tel: 01326 252100
www.condenastjohansens.com/budockvean

CORNWALL - FALMOUTH (MAWNAN SMITH)

Meudon Hotel

Mawnan Smith, Near Falmouth, Cornwall TR11 5HT

Tel: 01326 250541
www.condenastjohansens.com/meudon

Hotels - Great Britain & Ireland

Properties listed below can be found in our Recommended Hotels & Spas – Great Britain & Ireland 2012 Guide

CORNWALL - PORTLOE (ROSELAND PENINSULA)

The Lugger Hotel

Portloe, Near Truro, Cornwall TR2 5RD

Tel: 0844 414 6550
www.condenastjohansens.com/lugger

CUMBRIA - WINDERMERE

Gilpin Hotel & Lake House

Crook Road, Windermere, Cumbria LA23 3NE

Tel: 015394 88818
www.condenastjohansens.com/gilpinlodge

CORNWALL - ST AGNES (MITHIAN)

Rose-In-Vale Country House Hotel

Mithian, St Agnes, Cornwall TR5 0QD

Tel: 01872 552202
www.condenastjohansens.com/roseinvalecountryhouse

CUMBRIA - WINDERMERE

Holbeck Ghyll Country House Hotel

Holbeck Lane, Windermere, Cumbria LA23 1LU

Tel: 01539 432 375
www.condenastjohansens.com/holbeckghyll

CORNWALL - ST IVES

St Ives Harbour Hotel - Porthminster

The Terrace, St Ives, Cornwall TR26 2BN

Tel: 01736 795221
www.condenastjohansens.com/stivesharbour

CUMBRIA - WINDERMERE (BOWNESS)

Linthwaite House Hotel

Crook Road, Windermere, Cumbria LA23 3JA

Tel: 015394 88600
www.condenastjohansens.com/linthwaitehouse

CUMBRIA - BRAMPTON

Farlam Hall Hotel

Brampton, Cumbria CA8 2NG

Tel: 016977 46234
www.condenastjohansens.com/farlamhall

CUMBRIA - WINDERMERE (NEWBY BRIDGE)

Lakeside Hotel on Lake Windermere

Lakeside, Newby Bridge, Cumbria LA12 8AT

Tel: 015395 30001
www.condenastjohansens.com/lakeside

CUMBRIA - GRANGE-OVER-SANDS

Netherwood Hotel

Lindale Road, Grange-Over-Sands, Cumbria LA11 6ET

Tel: 015395 32552
www.condenastjohansens.com/netherwood

DERBYSHIRE - BASLOW

Fischer's Baslow Hall

Calver Road, Baslow, Derbyshire DE45 1RR

Tel: 01246 583259
www.condenastjohansens.com/fischers

CUMBRIA - KESWICK (BASSENTHWAITE LAKE)

Armathwaite Hall Country House Hotel and Spa

Bassenthwaite Lake, Keswick, Cumbria CA12 4RE

Tel: 017687 76551
www.condenastjohansens.com/armathwaite

DERBYSHIRE - RISLEY

Risley Hall Hotel and Spa

Derby Road, Risley, Derbyshire DE72 3SS

Tel: 0115 939 9000
www.condenastjohansens.com/risleyhall

CUMBRIA - KESWICK (BORROWDALE)

The Lodore Falls Hotel

Borrowdale, Keswick, Cumbria CA12 5UX

Tel: 017687 77285
www.condenastjohansens.com/lodorefalls

DEVON - BURRINGTON (NEAR BARNSTAPLE, UMBERLEIGH)

Northcote Manor Country House Hotel

Burrington, Umberleigh, Devon EX37 9LZ

Tel: 01769 560501
www.condenastjohansens.com/northcotemanor

CUMBRIA - KESWICK (LAKE THIRLMERE)

Dale Head Hall Lakeside Hotel

Thirlmere, Keswick, Cumbria CA12 4TN

Tel: 017687 72478
www.condenastjohansens.com/daleheadhall

DEVON - CHAGFORD

Gidleigh Park

Chagford, Devon TQ13 8HH

Tel: 01647 432367
www.condenastjohansens.com/gidleighpark

Hotels - Great Britain & Ireland

Properties listed below can be found in our Recommended Hotels & Spas – Great Britain & Ireland 2012 Guide

DEVON - EXETER (HONITON)

Combe House

Gittisham, Honiton, Near Exeter, Devon EX14 3AD

Tel: 01404 540400
www.condenastjohansens.com/combehousegittisham

DORSET - WAREHAM

The Priory Hotel

Church Green, Wareham, Dorset BH20 4ND

Tel: 01929 551666
www.condenastjohansens.com/priorywareham

DEVON - SALCOMBE (SOUTH SANDS)

The Tides Reach Hotel

South Sands, Salcombe, Devon TQ8 8LJ

Tel: 01548 843466
www.condenastjohansens.com/tidesreach

DURHAM - DARLINGTON (HURWORTH-ON-TEES)

Rockliffe Hall

Hurworth-on-Tees, Near Darlington, Durham DL2 2DU

Tel: 01325 729999
www.condenastjohansens.com/rockliffehall

DEVON - SIDMOUTH

Hotel Riviera

The Esplanade, Sidmouth, Devon EX10 8AY

Tel: 01395 515201
www.condenastjohansens.com/riviera

GLOUCESTERSHIRE - BIBURY

Bibury Court

Bibury, Gloucestershire GL7 5NT

Tel: 01285 740337
www.condenastjohansens.com/biburycourt

DEVON - WOOLACOMBE (MORTEHOE)

Watersmeet Hotel

Mortehoe, Woolacombe, Devon EX34 7EB

Tel: 01271 870333
www.condenastjohansens.com/watersmeet

GLOUCESTERSHIRE - CIRENCESTER (BARNSLEY)

Barnsley House

Barnsley, Cirencester, Gloucestershire GL7 5EE

Tel: 01285 740000
www.condenastjohansens.com/barnsleyhouse

DORSET - CHRISTCHURCH

Captains Club Hotel & Spa

Wick Ferry, Wick Lane, Christchurch, Dorset BH23 1HU

Tel: 01202 475111
www.condenastjohansens.com/captainsclubhotel

GLOUCESTERSHIRE - LOWER SLAUGHTER

Lower Slaughter Manor

Lower Slaughter, Gloucestershire GL54 2HP

Tel: 01451 820456
www.condenastjohansens.com/lowerslaughtermanor

DORSET - CHRISTCHURCH

Christchurch Harbour Hotel & Spa

95 Mudeford, Christchurch, Dorset BH23 3NT

Tel: 01202 483434
www.condenastjohansens.com/christchurchharbour

GLOUCESTERSHIRE - LOWER SLAUGHTER

Washbourne Court

Lower Slaughter, Gloucestershire GL54 2HS

Tel: 01451 822143
www.condenastjohansens.com/washbournecourt

DORSET - EVERSHOT (NEAR DORCHESTER)

Summer Lodge Country House Hotel, Restaurant and Spa

9 Fore Street, Evershot, Dorset DT2 0JR

Tel: 01935 482000
www.condenastjohansens.com/summerlodge

GLOUCESTERSHIRE - MINCHINHAMPTON

Burleigh Court

Burleigh, Minchinhampton, Near Stroud,
Gloucestershire GL5 2PF

Tel: 01453 883804
www.condenastjohansens.com/burleighgloucestershire

DORSET - LYME REGIS

Alexandra Hotel and Restaurant

Pound Street, Lyme Regis, Dorset DT7 3HZ

Tel: 01297 442010
www.condenastjohansens.com/hotelalexandra

GLOUCESTERSHIRE - MORETON-IN-MARSH (COTSWOLDS)

The Manor House Hotel

Moreton-in-marsh, Gloucestershire GL56 0LJ

Tel: 01608 650501
www.condenastjohansens.com/manorhousemoreton

Hotels - Great Britain & Ireland

Properties listed below can be found in our Recommended Hotels & Spas – Great Britain & Ireland 2012 Guide

GLOUCESTERSHIRE - TETBURY

Calcot Manor Hotel & Spa

Near Tetbury, Gloucestershire GL8 8YJ

Tel: 01666 890391
www.condenastjohansens.com/calcotmanor

LONDON - CHELSEA HARBOUR

The Wyndham Grand London Chelsea Harbour

Chelsea Harbour, London SW10 0XG

Tel: 020 7823 3000
www.condenastjohansens.com/wyndhamlondon

HAMPSHIRE - LYNDHURST

Lime Wood

Beaulieu Road, Lyndhurst, Hampshire SO43 7FZ

Tel: 023 8028 7177
www.condenastjohansens.com/limewood

LONDON - CITY

Cheval Calico House

42 Bow Lane, London EC4M 9DT

Tel: 020 7489 2500
www.condenastjohansens.com/calicohouse

HAMPSHIRE - NEW FOREST

Chewton Glen

New Milton, New Forest, Hampshire BH25 6QS

Tel: 01425 275341
www.condenastjohansens.com/chewtonglen

LONDON - EARLS COURT

The Mayflower Hotel

26-28 Trebovir Road, London SW5 9NJ

Tel: 020 7370 0991
www.condenastjohansens.com/mayflower

HAMPSHIRE - ROTHERWICK

Tylney Hall

Rotherwick, Hook, Hampshire RG27 9AZ

Tel: 01256 764881
www.condenastjohansens.com/tylneyhall

LONDON - EARLS COURT

Twenty Nevern Square

20 Nevern Square, London SW5 9PD

Tel: 020 7565 9555
www.condenastjohansens.com/twentynevernsquare

HEREFORDSHIRE - HEREFORD

Castle House

Castle Street, Hereford, Herefordshire HR1 2NW

Tel: 01432 356321
www.condenastjohansens.com/castlehse

LONDON - KENSINGTON

Cheval Gloucester Park

Ashburn Place, Kensington, London SW7 4LL

Tel: 020 7373 1444
www.condenastjohansens.com/gloucesterpark

LINCOLNSHIRE - STAMFORD

The George Of Stamford

St Martins, Stamford, Lincolnshire PE9 2LB

Tel: 01780 750750
www.condenastjohansens.com/georgeofstamford

LONDON - KENSINGTON

Cheval Thorney Court

Palace Gate, Kensington, London W8 5NJ

Tel: 020 7581 5324
www.condenastjohansens.com/thorneycourt

LONDON - BUCKINGHAM PALACE

41

41 Buckingham Palace Road, London SW1W 0PS

Tel: 020 7300 0041
www.condenastjohansens.com/
41buckinghampalaceroad

LONDON - KENSINGTON

Kensington House Hotel

15-16 Prince Of Wales Terrace, Kensington, London W8 5PQ

Tel: 020 7937 2345
www.condenastjohansens.com/kensingtonhouse

LONDON - CHELSEA

Cheval Phoenix House

1 Wilbraham Place, Sloane Street, London, SW1X 9AE

Tel: 020 7259 8222
www.condenastjohansens.com/phoenixhouse

LONDON - KENSINGTON

Milestone Hotel

1 Kensington Court, London W8 5DL

Tel: 020 7917 1000
www.condenastjohansens.com/milestone

Hotels - Great Britain & Ireland

Properties listed below can be found in our Recommended Hotels & Spas – Great Britain & Ireland 2012 Guide

LONDON - KNIGHTSBRIDGE

Beaufort House

45 Beaufort Gardens, Knightsbridge, London SW3 1PN

Tel: 020 7584 2600
www.condenastjohansens.com/
beauforthouseapartments

LONDON - WESTMINSTER

51 Buckingham Gate, Taj Suites and Residences

51 Buckingham Gate, Westminster, London SW1E 6AF

Tel: 020 7769 7766
www.condenastjohansens.com/buckinghamgate

LONDON - KNIGHTSBRIDGE

Cheval Knightsbridge

13 Cheval Place, London, SW7 1EW

Tel: 020 7225 3325
www.condenastjohansens.com/chevalknightsbridge

NORTHUMBERLAND - OTTERBURN

Otterburn Hall

Otterburn, Northumberland NE19 1HE

Tel: 01830 520663
www.condenastjohansens.com/otterburnhall

LONDON - KNIGHTSBRIDGE

The Egerton House Hotel

17-19 Egerton Terrace, Knightsbridge, London SW3 2BX

Tel: 020 7589 2412
www.condenastjohansens.com/egertonhouse

RUTLAND - OAKHAM

Hambleton Hall

Hambleton, Oakham, Rutland LE15 8TH

Tel: 01572 756991
www.condenastjohansens.com/hambletonhall

LONDON - MAYFAIR

The Mandeville Hotel

Mandeville Place, London W1U 2BE

Tel: 020 7935 5599
www.condenastjohansens.com/mandeville

SOMERSET - TAUNTON

The Castle at Taunton

Castle Green, Taunton, Somerset TA1 1NF

Tel: 01823 272671
www.condenastjohansens.com/castleattaunton

LONDON - MAYFAIR

The May Fair

Stratton Street, Mayfair, London W1J 8LT

Tel: 020 7769 4041
www.condenastjohansens.com/mayfair

STAFFORDSHIRE - LICHFIELD (HOAR CROSS)

Hoar Cross Hall Spa Resort

Hoar Cross, Near Yoxall, Staffordshire DE13 8QS

Tel: 01283 575671
www.condenastjohansens.com/hoarcrosshall

LONDON - MAYFAIR

Westbury Hotel

Bond Street, Mayfair, London W1S 2YF

Tel: 020 7629 7755
www.condenastjohansens.com/westburymayfair

EAST SUSSEX - EASTBOURNE

The Grand Hotel

King Edward's Parade, Eastbourne, East Sussex BN21 4EQ

Tel: 01323 412345
www.condenastjohansens.com/grandeastbourne

LONDON - NOTTING HILL

The New Linden Hotel

58 - 60 Leinster Square, Notting Hill, London W2 4PS

Tel: 020 7221 4321
www.condenastjohansens.com/newlindenhotel

EAST SUSSEX - FOREST ROW

Ashdown Park Hotel and Country Club

Wych Cross, Forest Row, East Sussex RH18 5JR

Tel: 01342 824988
www.condenastjohansens.com/ashdownpark

LONDON - PICCADILLY

Sofitel London St James

6 Waterloo Place, London SW1Y 4AN

Tel: 020 7747 2200
www.condenastjohansens.com/stjames

EAST SUSSEX - LEWES (LITTLE HORSTED)

Horsted Place Country House Hotel

Little Horsted, East Sussex TN22 5TS

Tel: 01825 750581
www.condenastjohansens.com/horstedplace

Hotels - Great Britain & Ireland

Properties listed below can be found in our Recommended Hotels & Spas – Great Britain & Ireland 2012 Guide

EAST SUSSEX - LEWES (NEWICK)

Newick Park

Newick, Near Lewes, East Sussex BN8 4SB

Tel: 01825 723633

www.condenastjohansens.com/newickpark

WARWICKSHIRE - SOLIHULL

Hampton Manor

Shadowbrook Lane, Hampton-in-Arden, Solihull, Warwickshire B92 0EN

Tel: 01675 446080

www.condenastjohansens.com/hamptonmanor

WEST SUSSEX - ARUNDEL (CLIMPING)

Bailiffscourt Hotel & Spa

Climping, Arundel, West Sussex BN17 5RW

Tel: 01903 723511

www.condenastjohansens.com/bailiffscourt

WARWICKSHIRE - STRATFORD-UPON-AVON

Welcombe Hotel Spa & Golf Club

Warwick Road, Stratford-upon-Avon, Warwickshire CV37 0NR

Tel: 01789 295252

www.condenastjohansens.com/welcombe

WEST SUSSEX - CUCKFIELD (NEAR GATWICK)

Ockenden Manor

Ockenden Lane, Cuckfield, West Sussex RH17 5LD

Tel: 01444 416111

www.condenastjohansens.com/ockendenmanor

WILTSHIRE - BATH (COLERNE)

Lucknam Park Hotel & Spa

Colerne, Chippenham, Wiltshire SN14 8AZ

Tel: 01225 742777

www.condenastjohansens.com/lucknampark

WEST SUSSEX - EAST GRINSTEAD (FELBRIDGE)

Felbridge Hotel & Spa

London Road, East Grinstead, West Sussex RH19 2BH

Tel: 01342 337700

www.condenastjohansens.com/felbridgehotel

WILTSHIRE - MALMESBURY

Whatley Manor

Easton Grey, Malmesbury, Wiltshire SN16 0RB

Tel: 01666 822888

www.condenastjohansens.com/whatley

WEST SUSSEX - MIDHURST

Park House Hotel & PH2O Spa

Bepton, Midhurst, West Sussex GU29 0JB

Tel: 01730 819 000

www.condenastjohansens.com/parkhousehotel

WORCESTERSHIRE - BROADWAY

Dormy House

Willersey Hill, Broadway, Worcestershire WR12 7LF

Tel: 01386 852711

www.condenastjohansens.com/dormyhouse

WEST SUSSEX - MIDHURST

The Spread Eagle Hotel & Spa

South Street, Midhurst, West Sussex GU29 9NH

Tel: 01730 816911

www.condenastjohansens.com/spreadeaglemidhurst

NORTH YORKSHIRE - HARROGATE

Rudding Park Hotel, Spa & Golf

Follifoot, Harrogate, North Yorkshire HG3 1JH

Tel: 01423 871 350

www.condenastjohansens.com/ruddingpark

WEST SUSSEX - WEST HOATHLY (NEAR EAST GRINSTEAD)

Gravetye Manor

Vowels Lane, Near West Hoathly, West Sussex RH19 4LJ

Tel: 01342 810567

www.condenastjohansens.com/gravetyemanor

NORTH YORKSHIRE - HAWES (UPPER WENSLEYDALE)

Simonstone Hall

Hawes, North Yorkshire DL8 3LY

Tel: 01969 667255

www.condenastjohansens.com/simonstonehall

WARWICKSHIRE - COVENTRY (BERKSWELL)

Nailcote Hall

Nailcote Lane, Berkswell, Near Solihull, Warwickshire CV7 7DE

Tel: 02476 466174

www.condenastjohansens.com/nailcotehall

CLARE - NEWMARKET-ON-FERGUS

Dromoland Castle

Newmarket-On-Fergus, Co Clare

Tel: 00 353 61368144

www.condenastjohansens.com/dromolandcastle

Hotels - Great Britain & Ireland

Properties listed below can be found in our Recommended Hotels & Spas – Great Britain & Ireland 2012 Guide

CORK - CORK

Castlemartyr Resort

Castlemartyr, Co Cork

Tel: 00 353 21 4219000
www.condenastjohansens.com/castlemartyr

ABERDEENSHIRE - CRAIGELLACHIE (BANFFSHIRE)

Craigellachie Hotel of Speyside

Craigellachie, Aberlour, Banffshire AB38 9SR

Tel: 01340 881204
www.condenastjohansens.com/craigellachie

CORK - FOTA ISLAND

Fota Island Hotel & Spa

Fota Island Resort, Fota Island, Co Cork

Tel: 00 353 21 488 3700
www.condenastjohansens.com/fotaisland

ARGYLL & BUTE - PORT APPIN

Airds Hotel

Port Appin, Appin, Argyll PA38 4DF

Tel: 01631 730236
www.condenastjohansens.com/airdshotel

GALWAY - CONNEMARA

Cashel House

Cashel, Connemara, Co Galway

Tel: 00 353 95 31001
www.condenastjohansens.com/cashelhouse

ARGYLL & BUTE - TARBERT

Stonefield Castle

Tarbert, Loch Fyne, Argyll PA29 6YJ

Tel: 01880 820836
www.condenastjohansens.com/stonefield

GALWAY - GALWAY

The g Hotel

Wellpark, Galway, Co Galway

Tel: 00 353 91 865 200
www.condenastjohansens.com/theghotel

EAST LOTHIAN - MUIRFIELD (GULLANE)

Greywalls and Chez Roux

Muirfield, Gullane, East Lothian EH31 2EG

Tel: 01620 842 144
www.condenastjohansens.com/greywalls

KERRY - KILLARNEY

Cahernane House Hotel

Muckross Road, Killarney, Co Kerry

Tel: 00 353 64 6631895
www.condenastjohansens.com/cahernane

HIGHLAND - FORT WILLIAM

Inverlochy Castle

Torlundy, Fort William PH33 6SN

Tel: 01397 702177
www.condenastjohansens.com/inverlochy

MAYO - CONG

Ashford Castle

Cong, Co Mayo

Tel: 00 353 94 95 46003
www.condenastjohansens.com/ashfordcastle

HIGHLAND - INVERNESS

Rocpool Reserve and Chez Roux

Culduthel Road, Inverness, IV2 4AG

Tel: 01463 240089
www.condenastjohansens.com/rocpool

MAYO - WESTPORT

Knockranny House Hotel & Spa

Westport, Co Mayo

Tel: 00 353 98 28600
www.condenastjohansens.com/knockranny

HIGHLAND - LOCHINVER (SUTHERLAND)

Inver Lodge Hotel and Chez Roux

Lochinver, Sutherland IV27 4LU

Tel: 01571 844496
www.condenastjohansens.com/inverlodge

WICKLOW - ENNISKERRY

The Ritz-Carlton, Powerscourt

Powerscourt Estate, Enniskerry, Co Wicklow

Tel: 00 353 1 274 8888
www.condenastjohansens.com/ritzcarlton

CONWY - LLANDUDNO

St Tudno Hotel & Restaurant

North Promenade, Llandudno, North Wales LL30 2LP

Tel: 01492 874411
www.condenastjohansens.com/sttudno

Hotels - Great Britain & Ireland

Properties listed below can be found in our Recommended Hotels & Spas – Great Britain & Ireland 2012 Guide

DENBIGHSHIRE - RUTHIN

Ruthin Castle Hotel

Ruthin, Denbighshire LL15 2NU

Tel: 01824 702664
www.condenastjohansens.com/ruthincastle

POWYS - LAKE VYRNWY

Lake Vyrnwy Hotel & Spa

Lake Vyrnwy, Llanwddyn, Powys SY10 0LY

Tel: 01691 870 692
www.condenastjohansens.com/lakevyrnwy

GWYNEDD - DOLGELLAU (PENMAENPOOL)

Penmaenuchaf Hall

Penmaenpool, Dolgellau, Gwynedd LL40 1YB

Tel: 01341 422129
www.condenastjohansens.com/penmaenuchafhall

POWYS - LLANGAMMARCH WELLS

Lake Country House & Spa

Llangammarch Wells, Powys LD4 4BS

Tel: 01591 620202
www.condenastjohansens.com/lakecountryhouse

PEMBROKESHIRE - NARBERTH

The Grove Hotel

Molleston, Narberth, Pembrokeshire SA67 8BX

Tel: 01834 860 915
www.condenastjohansens.com/grovenarberth

WILLIS&**GAMBIER**

Furniture designed for life

Because life is about choices

With a stunning portfolio of designs including, contemporary, classic French and rustic designs, Condé Nast Johansens preferred furniture supplier, Willis and Gambier, manufacture furniture that will add style and character to any setting

Visit www.wguk.com and be inspired!

www.wguk.com   +44 (0) 1733 318400

Historic Houses, Castles & Gardens

We are pleased to feature over 170 places to visit during your stay at a Condé Nast Johansens Recommendation.
More information about these attractions, including opening times and entry fees, can be found on www.historichouses.co.uk

Channel Islands

Guernsey

Sausmarez Manor – Sausmarez Road, St Martin, Guernsey GY4 6SG. Tel: 01481 235571

England

Bath & North East Somerset

Cothay Manor and Gardens – Greenham, Wellington, Bath & North East Somerset TA21 0JR. Tel: 01823 672283
Maunsel House – North Newton, Nr Taunton, Bath & North East Somerset TA7 0BU. Tel: 01278 661076

Bedfordshire

John Bunyan Museum & Library – Bunyan Meeting Free Church, Mill Street, Bedford, Bedfordshire MK40 3EU. Tel: 01234 270303
Moggerhanger Park – Park Road, Moggerhanger, Bedfordshire MK44 3RW. Tel: 01767 641007

Berkshire

Eton College – The Visits Office, Eton High Street, Windsor, Berkshire SL4 6DW. Tel: 01753 671177

Buckinghamshire

Nether Winchendon House – Nr Aylesbury, Buckinghamshire HP18 0DY. Tel: 01844 290101
Stowe House – Stowe, Buckinghamshire MK18 5EH. Tel: 01280 818166 24 Hour Recorded enquiries line / 01280 8181229 Office hour enquiries
Waddesdon Manor – Waddesdon, Nr Aylesbury, Buckinghamshire HP18 0JH. Tel: 01296 653226

Cambridgeshire

Island Hall – Post Street, Godmanchester, Cambridgeshire PE29 2BA. Tel: 01480 459676
The Manor – Hemingford Grey, Huntingdon, Cambridgeshire PE28 9BN. Tel: 01480 463134
Oliver Cromwell's House – 29 St Mary's Street, Ely, Cambridgeshire CB7 4HF. Tel: 01353 662062

Cheshire

Dorfold Hall – Nantwich, Cheshire CW5 8LD. Tel: 01270 625245
Norton Priory Museum & Garden – Tudor Road, Manor Park, Runcorn, Cheshire WA7 1SX. Tel: 01928 569895
Rode Hall and Gardens – Scholar Green, Cheshire ST7 3QP. Tel: 01270 882961 / 873237
Tabley House Collection – Knutsford, Cheshire WA16 0HB. Tel: 01565 750 151

Cornwall

Caerhays Castle – Estate Office, Gorran, St. Austell, Cornwall PL26 6LY. Tel: 01872 501310 /501144
Mount Edgcumbe House & Country Park – Cremyll, Torpoint, Cornwall PL10 1HZ. Tel: 01752 822236
Pencarrow House and Gardens – Washway, Bodmin, Cornwall PL30 3AG. Tel: 01208 841369
Port Eliot House – Port Eliot Estate Office, St Germans, Saltash, Cornwall PL12 5ND. Tel: 01503 230211
Prideaux Place – Padstow, Cornwall PL28 8RP. Tel: 01841 532411

Cumbria

Dove Cottage & The Wordsworth Museum – The Wordsworth Trust, Dove Cottage, Grasmere, Cumbria LA22 9SH. Tel: 015394 35544
Isel Hall – Cockermouth, Cumbria CA13 0QG. Tel: 01900 826127 / 812436
Townend – Troutbeck, Windermere, Cumbria LA23 1LB. Tel: 015394 32628

Derbyshire

Hardwick Hall, Gardens, Park & Mill – The National Trust, Doe Lea, Chesterfield, Derbyshire S44 5QJ. Tel: 01246 858400
Melbourne Hall & Gardens – Melbourne, Derbyshire DE73 8EN. Tel: 01332 862502
Renishaw Hall and Gardens – Nr Sheffield, Derbyshire S21 3WB. Tel: 01246 432210

Devon

Bowringsleigh – Kingsbridge, Devon TQ7 3LL. Tel: 01548 857648 / 01548 852014
Downes – Crediton, Devon EX17 3PL. Tel: 01363 775142
Powderham Castle – Kenton, Exeter, Devon EX6 8JQ. Tel: 01626 890243

Dorset

Chiffchaffs – Chaffeymoor, Bourton, Gillingham, Dorset SP8 5BY. Tel: 01747 840841
Moignes Court – Owermoigne, Dorchester, Dorset DT2 8HY. Tel: 01305 853300
Russell-Cotes Art Gallery & Museum – Russell-Cotes Road, East Cliff, Bournemouth, Dorset BH1 3AA. Tel: 01202 451858

Durham

Raby Castle – Staindrop, Darlington, Durham DL2 3AH. Tel: 01833 660 202

Essex

Hedingham Castle – Bayley Street, Castle Hedingham, Nr Halstead, Essex CO9 3DJ. Tel: 01787 460261
Ingatestone Hall – Hall Lane, Ingatestone, Essex CM4 9NR. Tel: 01277 353010

Gloucestershire

Cheltenham Art Gallery & Museum – Clarence Street, Cheltenham, Gloucestershire GL50 3JT. Tel: 01242 237431
Frampton Court – Frampton-on-Severn, Gloucester, Gloucestershire GL2 7DY. Tel: 01452 740698
Hardwicke Court – Nr Gloucester, Gloucestershire GL2 4RS. Tel: 01452 720212
Nature In Art - Wallsworth Hall – Wallsworth Hall, Main A38, Twigworth, Gloucestershire GL2 9PA. Tel: 01452 731422
Sezincote House & Garden – Moreton-in-Marsh, Gloucestershire GL56 9AW. Tel: 01386 700444

Hampshire

Avington Park – Winchester, Hampshire SO21 1DB. Tel: 01962 779260
Beaulieu – Beaulieu Enterprises Ltd, John Montagu Bldg, Hampshire SO42 7ZN. Tel: 01590 614680
Broadlands – Romsey, Hampshire SO51 9ZD. Tel: 01794 529750/ 741
Buckler's Hard – Beaulieu, Brockenhurst, Hampshire SO42 7XB. Tel: 01590 616203
Gilbert White's House & Garden & The Oates Collection – High Street, Selborne, Nr Alton, Hampshire GU34 3JH. Tel: 01420 511275
Greywell Hill House – Greywell, Hook, Hampshire RG29 1DG. Tel: 01256 703565

Isle of Wight

Deacons Nursery (H.H) – Moor View, Godshill, Isle of Wight PO38 3HW. Tel: 01983 840750 or 522243

Kent

Belmont House – Belmont Park, Throwley, Faversham, Kent ME13 0HH. Tel: 01795 890202
Cobham Hall – Cobham, Nr Gravesend, Kent DA12 3BL. Tel: 01474 823371
The Grange – Ramsgate, Kent CT11 9NY. Tel: 01628 825925
Hever Castle and Gardens – Nr Edenbridge, Kent TN8 7NG. Tel: 01732 861710
Leeds Castle and Gardens – Maidstone, Kent ME17 1PL. Tel: 01622 765400
Marle Place Garden and Gallery – Marle Place Road, Brenchley, Kent TN12 7HS. Tel: 01892 722304
Mount Ephraim Gardens – Staple Street, Hernhill, Nr Faversham, Kent ME13 9TX. Tel: 01227 751496
The New College of Cobham – Cobhambury Road, Cobham, Nr Gravesend, Kent DA12 3BG. Tel: 01474 812503
Riverhill Himalayan Gardens – Riverhill, Sevenoaks, Kent TN15 0RR. Tel: 01732 459777

Leicestershire

Stapleford Park – Stappleford Park, Nr Melton Mowbray, Leicestershire LE14 2EF. Tel: 01572 787000

Historic Houses, Castles & Gardens

We are pleased to feature over 170 places to visit during your stay at a Condé Nast Johansens Recommendation.
More information about these attractions, including opening times and entry fees, can be found on www.historichouses.co.uk

London

18 Stafford Terrace – 18 Stafford Terrace, London W8 7BH. Tel: 0207 612 3306
Burgh House & Hampshire Museum – New End Square, Hampstead, London NW3 1LT. Tel: 020 7431 0144
Handel House Museum – 25 Brook Street, London W1K 4HB. Tel: 020 7495 1685
Keats House – Wentworth Place, Keats Grove, Hampstead, London NW3 2RR. Tel: 020 7794 6829
Leighton House – 12 Holland Park Road, London W14 8LZ. Tel: 020 7602 3316
Pitzhanger Manor House – Walpole Park, Mattock Lane, Ealing, London W5 5EQ. Tel: 020 8825 9803
St Paul's Cathedral – The Chapter House, St Paul's Churchyard, London EC4M 8AD. Tel: 020 7246 8350
Spencer House – 27 St. James's Place, London SW1A 1NR. Tel: 020 7514 1958
Syon Park – Syon Park, Brentford, London TW8 8JF. Tel: 020 8560 0882

Merseyside

Lady Lever Art Gallery – Port Sunlight Village, Wirral, Liverpool, Merseyside CH62 5EQ. Tel: 0151 478 4136
Meols Hall – Churchtown, Southport, Merseyside PR9 7LZ. Tel: 01704 228326
Sudley House – Mossley Hill Road, Aigburth, Liverpool, Merseyside L18 8BX. Tel: 0151 724 3245

Norfolk

Fairhaven Woodland and Water Garden – School Road, South Walsham, Norwich, Norfolk NR13 6DZ. Tel: 01603 270449
Mannington Hall – Saxthorpe, Norfolk NR11 7BB. Tel: 01263 584175 / 268444
South Elmham Hall – Hall Lane, St Cross, Harleston, Norfolk IP20 OPY. Tel: 01986 782526
Walsingham Abbey Grounds and Shirehall Museum – Common Place, Little Walsingham, Norfolk NR22 6BP. Tel: 01328 820510

Northumberland

Alnwick Castle – Alnwick, Northumberland NE66 1NQ. Tel: 01665 510777/ 511100
Bamburgh Castle – Bamburgh, Northumberland ME69 7DF. Tel: 01668 214208 / 214515
Chipchase Castle & Gardens – Wark on Tyne, Hexham, Northumberland NE48 3NT. Tel: 01434 230203

Oxfordshire

Blenheim Palace – Woodstock, Oxfordshire OX20 1PX. Tel: 0800 849 6500 (24 hour recorded message)
Broughton Castle – Banbury, Oxfordshire OX15 5EB. Tel: 01295 276070
Kingston Bagpuize House – Abingdon, Oxfordshire OX13 5AX. Tel: 01865 820259
Mapledurham House & Watermill – Nr Reading, Oxfordshire RG4 7TR. Tel: 01189 723350
Stonor Park – Nr Henley-on-Thames, Oxfordshire RG9 6HF. Tel: 01491 638587
Sulgrave Manor – Manor Road, Sulgrave, Banbury, Oxfordshire OX17 2SD. Tel: 01295 760205
Wallingford Castle Gardens – Castle Street, Wallingford, Oxfordshire OX10 0AL. Tel: 01491 835373

Rutland

Exton Park – Oakham, Rutland LE15 8AN. Tel: 01572 812208

Shropshire

Hodnet Hall Gardens – Hodnet, Market Drayton, Shropshire TF9 3NN. Tel: 01630 685786
Ludlow Castle – Castle Square, Ludlow, Shropshire SY8 1AY. Tel: 01584 874465

Somerset

Glastonbury Abbey – Abbey Gatehouse, Magdalene Street, Glastonbury, Somerset BA6 9EL. Tel: 01458 832267
Great House Farm – Wells Road, Theale, Wedmore, Somerset BS28 4SJ. Tel: 01934 713133
Hestercombe Gardens – Cheddon Fitzpaine, Taunton, Somerset TA2 8LG. Tel: 01823 13923
Kentsford – Washford, Watchet, Somerset TA23 0JD. Tel: 01984 631307
No. 1 Royal Crescent – Bath, Somerset BA1 2LR. Tel: 01225 428126
Orchard Wyndham – Williton, Taunton, Somerset TA4 4HH. Tel: 01984 632309
Robin Hood's Hut – Halswell, Goathurst, Somerset. Tel: 01628 825925

Woodlands Castle – Woodlands, Ruishton, Taunton, Somerset TA3 5LU. Tel: 01823 444955

Staffordshire

Whitmore Hall – Whitmore, Nr Newcastle-under-Lyme, Staffordshire ST5 5HW. Tel: 01782 680478

Suffolk

Freston Tower – Near Ipswich, Suffolk IP9 1AD. Tel: 01628 825925
Kentwell Hall – Long Melford, Sudbury, Suffolk CO10 9BA. Tel: 01787 310207
Otley Hall – Hall Lane, Otley, Nr Ipswich, Suffolk IP6 9PA. Tel: 01473 890264

Surrey

Claremont Fan Court School – Claremont Drive, Esher, Surrey KT10 9LY. Tel: 01372 473707
Guildford Castle – Castle Street, Guildford, Surrey, Surrey GU1 3TU. Tel: 01483 444751
Guildford House Gallery – 155 High Street, Guildford, Surrey GU1 3AJ. Tel: 01483 444751
Painshill Park Landscape Garden – Portsmouth Road, Cobham, Surrey KT11 1JE. Tel: 01932 868113
Ramster Gardens – Ramster, Chiddingfold, Surrey GU8 4SN. Tel: 01428 654167
Titsey Place and Gardens – Titsey, Oxted, Surrey RH8 0SD. Tel: 01273 475411

East Sussex

Bentley Wildfowl & Motor Museum – Halland, Nr Lewes, East Sussex BN8 5AF. Tel: 01825 840573
Firle Place – Nr Lewes, East Sussex BN8 6LP. Tel: 01273 858307
Gardens and Grounds of Herstmonceux Castle – Hailsham, East Sussex BN27 1RN. Tel: 01323 834444
Great Dixter House, Gardens & Nurseries – Great Dixter, Northiam, Rye, East Sussex TN31 6PH. Tel: 01797 252878
Merriments Gardens – Hawkhurst Road, Hurst Green, East Sussex TN19 7RA. Tel: 01580 860666
Pashley Manor Gardens – Ticehurst, East Sussex TN5 7HE. Tel: 01580 200888
Wilmington Priory – Wilmington, Nr Eastbourne, East Sussex BN26 5SW. Tel: 01628 825925

West Sussex

Arundel Castle – Arundel, West Sussex BN18 9AB. Tel: 01903 882173
Borde Hill – Borde Hill Lane, Haywards Heath, West Sussex RH16 1XP. Tel: 01444 450326
Cowdray – Visitor Centre, River Ground Stables, Midhurst, West Sussex GU29 9AL. Tel: 01730 810781
Denmans Garden – Denmans Lane, Fontwell, West Sussex BN18 0SU. Tel: 01243 542808
Goodwood House – Goodwood, Chichester, West Sussex PO18 0PX. Tel: 01243 755000 / 755048
High Beeches Gardens – Handcross, West Sussex RH17 6HQ. Tel: 01444 400589
Parham House & Gardens – Parham Park, Storrington, Nr Pulborough, West Sussex RH20 4HS. Tel: 01903 742021

Warwickshire

Arbury Hall – Nuneaton, Warwickshire CV10 7PT. Tel: 02476 382804

West Midlands

The Barber Institute of Fine Arts – University of Birmingham, Edgbaston, Birmingham, West Midlands B15 2TS. Tel: 0121 414 7333
The Birmingham Botanical Gardens & Glasshouses – Westbourne Road, Edgbaston, Birmingham, West Midlands B15 3TR. Tel: 0121 454 1860

Wiltshire

Iford Manor: The Peto Gardens – Bradford-on-Avon, Wiltshire BA15 2BA. Tel: 01225 863 146

Worcestershire

Harvington Hall – Harvington, Kidderminster, Worcestershire DY10 4LR. Tel: 01562 777846
Spetchley Park Gardens – Spetchley Park, Worcestershire WR5 1RS. Tel: 01453 810303

Historic Houses, Castles & Gardens

We are pleased to feature over 170 places to visit during your stay at a Condé Nast Johansens Recommendation.
More information about these attractions, including opening times and entry fees, can be found on www.historichouses.co.uk

North Yorkshire

Allerton Castle – Allerton Castle, Allerton Mauleverer, Knaresborough, North Yorkshire HG5 0SE. Tel: 01423 330 927
Brockfield Hall – Warthill, York, North Yorkshire YO19 5XJ. Tel: 01904 489 362
The Forbidden Corner – Tupgill Park Estate, Coverham, Nr Middleham, North Yorkshire DL8 4TJ. Tel: 01969 640638
Fountains Abbey and Studley Royal Water Garden – Ripon , Nr Harrogate, North Yorkshire HG4 3DY. Tel: 01765 608888
Kiplin Hall – Nr Scorton, Richmond, North Yorkshire. Tel: 01748 818178
Newby Hall and Gardens – Ripon, North Yorkshire HG4 5AE. Tel: Information Hotline: 0845 4504068Estate Office: 01423322583
Skipton Castle – Skipton, North Yorkshire BD23 1AW. Tel: 01756 792442

South Yorkshire

Epworth Old Rectory – Epworth, Doncaster, South Yorkshire DN9 1HX. Tel: 01427 872268

West Yorkshire

Ledston Hall – Hall Lane, Ledston, Castleford, West Yorkshire WF10 2BB. Tel: 01423 523 423
Shibden Hall – Listers Road, Halifax, West Yorkshire HX3 6XG. Tel: 01422 352246

Northern Ireland

Co Down

Mount Stewart House and Gardens – Portaferry Road, Newtownards, Co Down BT22 2AD. Tel: 028 4278 8387/028 4278 7817

Ireland

Cork

Bantry House & Garden – Bantry, Cork. Tel: 00 353 2 750 047
Blarney Castle, House and Garden – Blarney, Cork. Tel: 00 353 21 4385252

Kildare

The Irish National Stud – The Irish National Stud, Tully, kildare town , Kildare. Tel: 00 353 45 521617

Offaly

Birr Castle Demesne – Birr, Offaly. Tel: 00 353 5791 20336

Wicklow

Mount Usher Gardens – Ashford, Wicklow. Tel: 00 353 40440205

Scotland

Aberdeenshire

Arbuthnott House – Arbuthnott, Laurencekirk, Aberdeenshire AB30 1PA. Tel: 01561 320417
Duff House – Banff, Aberdeenshire AB45 3SX. Tel: 01261 818181
Provost Skene's House – Guestrow (off Broad Street), Aberdeen, Aberdeenshire AB10 1AS. Tel: 01224 641086

Angus

Brechin Castle – Brechin, Angus DD9 6SG. Tel: 01356 624566

Ayrshire

Kelburn Castle and Country Centre – Kelburn, Fairlie (Nr Largs), Ayrshire KA29 0BE. Tel: 01475 568685

North Ayrshire

Auchinleck House – Ochiltree, North Ayrshire. Tel: 01628 825925

East Lothian

Lennoxlove House – Lennoxlove Estate, Haddington, East Lothian EH41 4NZ. Tel: 01620 823720

Dumfries & Galloway

Ardwell Gardens – Ardwell House, Ardwell, Stranraer, Dumfries & Galloway DG9 9LY. Tel: 01776 860227
Castle Kennedy Gardens – The Estates Office, Rephad, Stranraer, Dumfries & Galloway DG9 8BX. Tel: 01776 702 024
Gilnockie Tower – 7 Riverside Park, , Canonbie , Dumfriesshire, Dumfries & Galloway DG14 0UY. Tel: 01387 371876
Glenmalloch Lodge – Newton Stewart, Dumfries & Galloway. Tel: 01628 825925

Highland

Clan Donald Skye – Armadale, Sleat, Isle of Skye, Highland IV45 8RS. Tel: 01471 844305
Dunvegan Castle & Gardens – The MacLeod Estate Office, Dunvegan, Isle of Skye, Highland IV55 8WF. Tel: 01470 521206
Mount Stuart – Mount Stuart, Isle of Bute, Highland PA20 9LR. Tel: 01700 503877
Scone Palace – Scone, Perth, Perthshire, Highland PH2 6BD. Tel: 01738 552300

Scottish Borders

Abbotsford Gardens and Visitors Centre – Melrose, Roxburghshire, Scottish Borders TD6 9BQ. Tel: 01896 752 043
Floors Castle – Kelso, Scottish Borders TD5 7SF. Tel: 01573 223333
Manderston – Duns, Berwickshire, Scottish Borders TD11 3PP. Tel: 01361 883 450
Mellerstain House – The Mellerstain Trust, Gordon, Berwickshire, Scottish Borders TD3 6LG. Tel: 01573 410225
Paxton House, Gallery & Country Park – Paxton, Nr Berwick upon Tweed, Scottish Borders TD15 1SZ. Tel: 01289 386291
Traquair House – Innerleithen, Peebles, Scottish Borders EH44 6PW. Tel: 01896 830 323

Wales

Denbighshire

Dolbelydr – Trefnant, Denbighshire. Tel: 01628 825925

Flintshire

Golden Grove – Llanasa, Nr Holywell, Flintshire CH8 9NA. Tel: 01745 854452

Gwynedd

Portmeirion Village & Gardens – Portmeirion Village, Portmeirion, Gwynedd LL48 6ER. Tel: (01766) 770000

Monmouthshire

Llanvihangel Court – Nr Abergavenny, Monmouthshire NP7 8DH. Tel: 01873 890 217 / 0208 947 9188
Usk Castle – Castle House, Monmouth Rd, Usk, Monmouthshire NP15 1SD. Tel: 01291 672563

Newport

Tredegar House & Park – Newport NP10 8YW. Tel: 01633 815880

Pembrokeshire

St David's Cathedral – The Deanery, The Close, St Davids, Pembrokeshire SA62 6RH. Tel: 01437 720 202

Powys

The Judge's Lodging – Broad Street, Presteigne, Mid Wales, Powys LD8 2AD. Tel: 01544 260650

France

Loire Valley

Château de Chenonceau – 37150 Chenonceaux, Loire Valley, France 37150. Tel: 00 33 2 47 23 44 02

Normandy

Chateau de Martinvast and Floral Park – Domaine de Beaurepaire, 50690 Martinvast, Basse-Normandie, France 50690. Tel: 00 33 2 33 87 20 80

Hotels, Europe & The Mediterranean

All the properties listed below can be found in our Recommended Hotels & Spas, Europe & The Mediterranean 2012 Guide.

Austria

Hotel the Crystal .... Tirol ....+43 5 256 6454

Belgium

Manoir du Dragon ....Knokke~Heist ....+32 50 63 05 80
Hotel Damier Kortrijk ....Kortrijk ....+32 56 22 15 47
Hostellerie Ter Driezen...........................Turnhout ....+32 14 41 87 57

Channel Islands

The Atlantic Hotel .... Jersey...........................+44 1534 744101

Croatia

Kazbek ....Dubrovnik ....+385 20 362 900
Villa Dubrovnik...Dubrovnik ....+385 20 500 300
Hotel Heritage Martinis Marchi ....Solta Island............................+385 21 572 768

Egypt

Farah Nile Cruise.......................................Luxor - Aswan ....+202 2418 5456/86

France

Hostellerie Les Bas Rupts Le Chalet Fleuri...
....Alsace~Lorraine...................+33 3 29 63 09 25
Hôtel à la Cour d'Alsace ....Alsace~Lorraine...................+33 3 88 95 07 00
Hôtel Les Têtes...Alsace~Lorraine...............+33 3 89 24 43 43
Romantik Hôtel le Maréchal................Alsace~Lorraine...................+33 3 89 41 60 32
Domaine de Rochevilaine....................Brittany ....+33 2 97 41 61 61
Ti al Lannec & Spa ....Brittany ....+33 2 96 15 01 01
Abbaye de la Bussière ....Burgundy - Franche~Comté ....
....+33 3 80 49 02 29
Château Hôtel André Ziltener ....Burgundy - Franche~Comté ....
....+33 3 80 62 41 62
Ermitage de Corton.................................Burgundy - Franche~Comté ....
....+33 3 80 22 05 28
La Borde ....Burgundy - Franche~Comté ....
....+33 3 86 47 69 01
Château d'Etoges....................................Champagne~Ardenne .....+33 3 26 59 30 08
Château de Fère.......................................Champagne~Ardenne .....+33 3 23 82 21 13

Domaine du Château de Barive ... Champagne~Ardenne.+33 3 23 22 15 15
Hôtel Le Pinarello.....................................Corsica.......................................+33 4 95 71 44 39
Château Eza...Côte d'Azur..............................+33 4 93 41 12 24
Hôtel Le Bailli de Suffren........................Côte d'Azur..............................+33 4 98 04 47 00
La Ferme d'Augustin ....Côte d'Azur..............................+33 4 94 55 97 00
La Villa Mauresque..................................Côte d'Azur..............................+33 494 83 02 42
Le Spinaker ....Languedoc~Roussillon..... +33 4 66 53 36 37
Château de l'Abbaye...............................Loire Valley ....+33 251 56 17 56
Le Manoir Saint Thomas ....Loire Valley ....+33 2 47 23 21 82
Château la Chenevière...........................Normandy ....+33 2 31 51 25 25
Carlton Hôtel...North~Picardy ....+33 3 20 13 33 13

Hotels, Europe & The Mediterranean

All the properties listed below can be found in our Recommended Hotels & Spas, Europe & The Mediterranean 2012 Guide.

Hospes Lancaster	Paris	+33 1 40 76 40 76
Hotel Banke	Paris	+33 1 55 33 22 22
Hôtel de Buci	Paris	+33 1 55 42 74 74
Hôtel Duc de Saint~Simon	Paris	+33 1 44 39 20 20

Hotel La Belle Juliette	**Paris**	**+33 1 42 22 97 40**
Hôtel San Régis	Paris	+33 1 44 95 16 16
Les Pléiades	Paris Region	+33 1 60 66 40 25
Chalet Hôtel Kaya	Rhône~Alpes	+33 4 79 41 42 00
Chalet Hôtel La Marmotte, Ski, Golf & Spa		
	Rhône~Alpes	+33 4 50 75 80 33
Château de Bagnols	Rhône~Alpes	+33 4 74 71 40 00
Domaine des Avenières	Rhône~Alpes	+33 4 50 44 02 23
Le Beau Rivage	Rhône~Alpes	+33 4 74 56 82 82
Le Fer à Cheval	Rhône~Alpes	+33 4 50 21 30 39
Le Portetta	Rhône~Alpes	+33 4 79 08 01 47
Château de Mirambeau	South West	+33 5 46 04 91 20
Hôtel du Palais	South West	+33 5 59 41 64 00

Villa La Tosca	**South West**	**+33 556 60 29 86**

Germany

Aspria Spa + Sporting Club + Hotel	Berlin	+49 30 890 68 88 68

Great Britain

Beaufort House	England	+44 20 7584 2600
The French Horn	England	+44 1189 692 204

The May Fair	**England**	**+44 20 7769 3046**
The Mayflower Hotel	England	+44 20 7370 0991
The New Linden Hotel	England	+44 20 7221 4321
Twenty Nevern Square	England	+44 20 7565 9555

Greece

Argentikon Luxury Suites	Chios	+30 22710 33111
Domes of Elounda, All Suites and Villas Spa Resort		
	Crete	+30 2310 810624
Pleiades Luxurious Villas	Crete	+30 2310 810624
Apanema Resort	Mykonos	+30 22890 28590

Tharroe of Mykonos	**Mykonos**	**+30 22890 27370**
Naxian Collection Luxury Villas and Suites		
	Naxos	+30 228 502 4300

All the properties listed below can be found in our Recommended Hotels & Spas, Europe & The Mediterranean 2012 Guide.

Petra Hotel & Suites.................................Patmos..............................+30 22470 34020
9 Muses Santorini Resort ....Santorini..........................+30 228 608 1781

Andronis Luxury Suites................. Santorini................**+30 22860 72041/2/3**
Astra Suites ....Santorini...................................+30 22860 23641
Petit Palace...Santorini...................+30 22860 23949/23944
Santorini Icons Hotel ....Santorini..............................+30 228 602 8950
Timedrops Santorini ....Santorini........................+30 2 28 60 83 282
White Santorini ....Santorini..............................+30 22860 25257
Lesante Hotel & Spa ....Zakynthos...........................+30 2 69 50 41 330

Italy

Hotel Punta Tragara.......................... Campania ....**+39 081 8370844**
Hotel Posta (Historical Residence) .....Emilia Romagna.................+39 05 22 43 29 44
Palazzo Dalla Rosa Prati ....Emilia Romagna....................+39 0521 386 429
Buonanotte Garibaldi ....Lazio....................................+39 06 58 330 733
Casa Montani - Luxury Town House .Lazio..+39 06 3260 0421
Hotel dei Borgognoni............................Lazio.......................................+39 06 6994 1505
Hotel dei Consoli ....Lazio...+39 0668 892 972
La Posta Vecchia ....Lazio .... +39 0699 49501

Palazzo Manfredi ....Lazio ....+39 06 77591380
Residenza Napoleone III........................Lazio....................................+39 3477 337 098
Villa Spalletti Trivelli..............................Lazio....................................+39 06 48907934
Abbadia San Giorgio - Historical Residence ....
                                                                  Liguria ....+39 0185 491119
Eight Hotel Paraggi ....Liguria.................................+39 0185 289961
Eight Hotel Portofino.............................Liguria............................... +39 0185 26991
Grand Hotel Bristol Resort & Spa.......Liguria ....+ 39 0185 273 313
Grand Hotel Diana Majestic.................Liguria...............................+39 0183 402 727
Grand Hotel Miramare ....Liguria.................................+39 0185 287013
Hotel Punta Est.......................................Liguria .... +39 019 600611
Hotel Vis à Vis ....Liguria .... +39 0185 42661
Bagni di Bormio Spa Resort.................Lombardy ....+39 0342 910131
Camperio House Suites and Apartments...
                                                                  Lombardy ....+39 02 303 22800
Grand Hotel Gardone Riviera...............Lombardy .... +39 0365 20261
Hotel Bellerive ....Lombardy......................+39 0365 520 410
Hotel de la Ville & La Villa ....Lombardy ....+39 039 39421
L'Albereta ....Lombardy......................+39 030 7760 550
Excelsior Hotel..Marche ....+39 0721 630011
Albergo L'Ostelliere ....Piemonte ....+39 0143 607 801
Relais Bella Rosina..................................Piemonte ....+39 011 9233600
Relais San Maurizio..................................Piemonte ....+39 0141 841900
Hotel Lucrezia ....Sardinia...............................+39 0783 412078
Hotel Relais Villa del Golfo & Spa.......Sardinia.......................+ 39 0789 892091
Petra Segreta Resort & SPA ....Sardinia.........................+39 0789 187 6441
Villa Las Tronas Hotel & Spa ....Sardinia .... +39 079 981 818

Baia Taormina Grand Palace Hotels & Spa ....
                                                                  Sicily...............................**+39 0942 756292**
Donna Carmela Resort ....Sicily .... +39 095 809383
Hotel Signum..Sicily ....+39 090 9844222
Hotel Villa Ducale ....Sicily .... +39 0942 28153
Locanda Don Serafino ....Sicily ....+39 0932 220065
Palazzo Failla Hotel.................................Sicily ....+39 0932 941059
Villa Carlotta ....Sicily ....+39 0942 626058
Castel Fragsburg.....................................Trentino - Alto Adige / Dolomites.....................
                                                                  +39 0473 244071
Du Lac et Du Parc Grand Resort.........Trentino - Alto Adige / Dolomites.....................
                                                                  +39 0464 566600
feldmilla. designhotel ....Trentino - Alto Adige / Dolomites.....................
                                                                  +39 0474 677100
GranPanorama Hotel Miramonti.......Trentino - Alto Adige / Dolomites....................
                                                                  +39 0473 27 9335

Hotels, Europe & The Mediterranean

All the properties listed below can be found in our Recommended Hotels & Spas, Europe & The Mediterranean 2012 Guide.

Hotel Ciasa Salares.....................Trentino - Alto Adige / Dolomites....................
+39 0471 849445

Hotel Gardena Grödnerhof........... Trentino - Alto Adige / Dolomites.............
+39 0471 796 315

Lido Palace ....Trentino - Alto Adige / Dolomites......................
+39 0464 021899

Parkhotel Holzner ....Trentino - Alto Adige / Dolomites......................
+39 0471 345 231

Albergo Pietrasanta - Palazzo Barsanti Bonetti.....................................
Tuscany ....+39 0584 793 727

Albergo Villa Casanova .... Tuscany.........................+39 0583 369000

Borgo Scopeto Relais ....Tuscany...................+39 0577 320001

Castello del Nero Hotel & Spa.............Tuscany.................... +39 055 806 470

Country House Casa Cornacchi ....Tuscany...................... +39 055 998229

Country Relais Villa L'Olmo..................Tuscany..................+39 055 23 11 311

Granduomo Charming Accommodation.......................................
Tuscany ....+39 055 267 0004

Hotel Byron..............................Tuscany...................+39 0584 787 052

Hotel Plaza e de Russie ....Tuscany .... +39 0584 44449

Hotel Tornabuoni Beacci...............Tuscany .... +39 055 212645

Il Bottaccio di Montignoso.................Tuscany...................+39 0585 340031

Il Pellicano Hotel ....Tuscany...................+39 0564 858111

L'Andana.............................Tuscany...................+39 0564 944 800

Lucignanello Bandini (Borgo Storico) ....
Tuscany ....+39 0577 803 068

Marignolle Relais & Charme.................Tuscany...................+39 055 228 6910

Monsignor Della Casa Country Resort & Spa..
Tuscany .... +39 055 840 821

Palazzo Carletti.............................Tuscany...................+39 0578 756080

Palazzo Magnani Feroni - all-suites florence ....
Tuscany ....+39 055 2399544

Palazzo San Lorenzo ....Tuscany...................+39 0577 923675

Petriolo Spa Resort ....Tuscany...................+39 0564 9091

Relais Borgo San Felice ....Tuscany...................+39 0577 3964

Relais la Suvera (Dimora Storica).......Tuscany...................+39 0577 960 300

Relais Villa Belpoggio (Historical House)....................................
Tuscany ....+39 055 9694411

Residenza del Moro.......................Tuscany................... +39 055 290884

Tenuta San Pietro Luxury Hotel & Restaurant.......................................
Tuscany ....+39 0583 926676

Tombolo Talasso Resort.......................Tuscany................... +39 0565 74530

Villa Armena, Relais & Beauty Farm...Tuscany...................+39 331 61 88 767

Villa Campestri Olive Oil Resort ....Tuscany...................+39 055 849 0107

Villa Curina Resort...........................Tuscany...................+39 0577 355630

Villa le Barone ....Tuscany................... +39 055 852621

Castello di Petroia ....Umbria ....+39 075 92 02 87

L'Antico Forziere Restaurant & Country Inn ....
Umbria ....+39 075 972 4314

Romantik Hotel Jolanda Sport ....Valle d'Aosta ....+39 0125 366 140

Albergo Quattro Fontane - Residenza d'Epoca ....
Veneto ....+39 041 526 0227

Ca Maria Adele ....Veneto...................+39 041 52 03 078

Ca' Sagredo Hotel.............................Veneto...................+39 041 2413111

Color Hotel style & design...................Veneto...................+39 045 621 0857

Hotel Caesius Thermae & SPA Resort ....
Veneto ....+39 045 7219100

Locanda San Vigilio ....Veneto...................+39 045 725 66 88

Londra Palace ....Veneto...................+39 041 5200533

Palazzo Selvadego ....Veneto...................+ 39 041 5200211

Park Hotel Brasilia.......................... Veneto ....+39 0421 380851

Relais Corte Guastalla ....Veneto...................+39 045 6095614

Relais la Magioca.............................Veneto...................+39 045 600 0167

Villa Cordevigo ....Veneto...................+39 045 723 5287

Hotels, Europe & The Mediterranean

All the properties listed below can be found in our Recommended Hotels & Spas, Europe & The Mediterranean 2012 Guide.

Morocco

Kasbah Du Toubkal................................High Atlas Mountains.......+212 524 48 56 11
Dar Azawad ....M'hamid...............................+212 524 84 87 30

Riad Enija .... Marrakech - Medina...+212 5 24 44 09 26
La Gazelle d'Or................................Taroudant.............................+212 528 852 039

The Netherlands

Ambassade Hotel...........................Amsterdam.............................. +31 20 5550 222

Portugal

Longevity Wellness Resort Monchique...
Algarve................................+351 282 240 110
Tivoli Marina Vilamoura.......................Algarve............................+351 289 303 303
Tivoli Victoria....................................Algarve............................+351 289 31 7000
Altis Belém Hotel & Spa.....................Lisbon & Tagus Valley ....+351 210 400 200

As Janelas Verdes............................ Lisbon & Tagus Valley +351 21 39 68 143
Heritage Av Liberdade............................Lisbon & Tagus Valley ....+351 213 404 040

Hotel Albatroz...Lisbon & Tagus Valley ....+351 21 484 73 80
Hotel Britania ....Lisbon & Tagus Valley ....+351 21 31 55 016
Lisboa Plaza Hotel...................................Lisbon & Tagus Valley ....+351 213 218 218
Palácio Estoril, Hotel, Golf & Spa........Lisbon & Tagus Valley .....+351 21 464 80 00
Solar do Castelo ....Lisbon & Tagus Valley ....+351 218 806 050
Tivoli Palácio de Seteais......................Lisbon & Tagus Valley ....+351 219 233 200
The Yeatman Hotel ....Oporto & Northern Portugal.........................
+351 22 013 3100

Spain

Barceló la Bobadilla...................................Andalucía................................ +34 958 32 18 61
DDG Luxury Retreat.....................................Andalucía................................ +34 629 657 203

Don Carlos Leisure Resort & Spa .. Andalucía ....+34 952 76 88 00
El Ladrón de Agua....................................Andalucía................................ +34 958 21 50 40
Gran Meliá Colón....................................Andalucía................................ +34 954 50 55 99
Gran Meliá Don Pepe Hotel ....Andalucía................................ +34 952 770 300
Hacienda Benazuza.................................Andalucía................................ +34 955 70 33 44
Hospes las Casas del Rey de Baeza....Andalucía................................ +34 954 561 496
Hospes Palacio de los Patos................Andalucía................................ +34 958 535 790
Hospes Palacio del Bailío ....Andalucía................................ +34 957 498 993
La Almoraima Hotel ....Andalucía................................ +34 956 693 002

Vincci Selección Estrella del Mar .. Andalucía .... +34 951 053 970
Vincci Seleccion Posada del Patio ......Andalucía................................ +34 951 001 020
Blau Porto Petro Beach Resort & Spa..Balearic Islands..........................+34 971 648 282
Can Lluc...Balearic Islands.......................+34 971 198 673
Cas Gasi ....Balearic Islands.......................+34 971 197 700
Cases de Son Barbassa..........................Balearic Islands.......................+34 971 565 776

Hotels, Europe & The Mediterranean

All the properties listed below can be found in our Recommended Hotels & Spas, Europe & The Mediterranean 2012 Guide.

Gran Hotel Son Net ....Balearic Islands....................... +34 971 14 70 00
Hospes Maricel.............................Balearic Islands....................... +34 971 707 744

Hotel Sant Joan de Binissaida ...... Balearic Islands..............+34 971 35 55 98
Hotel Ses Pitreras.......................Balearic Islands....................... +34 971 345 000
Son Granot...................................Balearic Islands....................... +34 971 355 555
Gran Hotel Atlantis Bahía Real............Canary Islands....................... +34 928 53 64 44
Gran Hotel Bahía del Duque Resort ..Canary Islands........................ +34 922 746 900
Hotel Botánico & The Oriental Spa Garden..
                                    Canary Islands....................... +34 922 38 14 00
Vincci Selección La Plantacion del Sur..
                                    Canary Islands....................... +34 922 717 773
La Almazara de Valdeverdeja..............Castilla~La Mancha.............. +34 925 454 804
Dolce Sitges................................Cataluña .... +34 938 109 000

Hotel 1898 .... Cataluña ....+34 93 552 95 52
Hotel Bagués................................Cataluña .... +34 93 34 35 000
Hotel Casa Fuster........................Cataluña .... +34 93 255 30 00

Hotel Duquesa de Cardona ....Cataluña................................... +34 93 268 90 90
Hotel Guitart Monterrey ....Cataluña................................... +34 972 34 60 54
Hotel Omm ....Cataluña................................... +34 93 445 40 00
Hotel Rigat Park & Spa Beach Hotel ..Cataluña.................................. +34 972 36 52 00
Hotel Santa Marta.............................Cataluña................................... +34 972 364 904
Hotel Vistabella ....Cataluña................................... +34 972 25 62 00
Hotel Etxegana Charming Hotel & Spa ....
                                    País Vasco................... +34 946 338 448
Barceló Asia Gardens Hotel & Thai Spa...
                                    Valencia.................... +34 966 818 400
El Rodat Hotel ....Valencia.................................... +34 966 470 710
Hotel Termas Marinas el Palasiet ....Valencia .... +34 964 300 250
Hotel Villa Marisol ....Valencia .... +34 96 587 57 00

Switzerland

Hotel Guarda Golf...........................Crans~Montana................... +41 27 486 2000
LeCrans Hotel & Spa........................Crans~Montana................... +41 27 486 60 60

Park Hotel Weggis........................... Weggis ....+41 41 392 05 05
CERVO Mountain Boutique Resort....Zermatt.................................... +41 27 968 12 12

Turkey

Cornelia Diamond Golf Resort and Spa ....
                                    Antalya....................................+90 242 710 1600
Kempinski Hotel Barbaros Bay ....Bodrum....................................+90 252 311 03 03
Gardens of Babylon Suites & Residence..
                                    Bodrum - Turgutreis ....+90 252 382 8217
Argos in Cappadocia ....Cappadocia - Uçhisar..........+90 384 2193130
Sacred House...................................Cappadocia - Ürgüp...........+90 384 341 7102
A'jia Hotel...Istanbul...................................+90 216 413 9300
Neorion Hotel ....Istanbul...................................+90 212 527 9090
Sumahan On The Water ....Istanbul...................................+90 216 422 8000
Villa Mahal...Kalkan....................................+90 242 844 32 68
Golden Key Bördübet.........................Marmaris ....+90 252 436 92 30

Hotels - The Americas

Properties listed below can be found in our Recommended Hotels, Inns, Resorts & Spas – The Americas, Atlantic, Caribbean & Pacific 2012 Guide

CANADA - BRITISH COLUMBIA (VANCOUVER)

Wedgewood Hotel & Spa

845 Hornby Street, Vancouver, British Columbia
V6Z 1V1

Tel: +1 604 689 7777
www.condenastjohansens.com/wedgewoodbc

CANADA - BRITISH COLUMBIA (VICTORIA)

The Magnolia Hotel & Spa

623 Courtney Street, Victoria, British Columbia
V8W 1B8

Tel: +1 250 381 0999
www.condenastjohansens.com/magnoliahotel

CANADA - NOVA SCOTIA (EAST KEMPTVILLE)

Trout Point Lodge of Nova Scotia

189 Trout Point Road, Off the East Branch Road and
Highway 203, East Kemptville, Nova Scotia B0W 1Y0

Tel: +1 902 761 2142
www.condenastjohansens.com/troutpoint

CANADA - BRITISH COLUMBIA (SONORA ISLAND)

Sonora Resort

Sonora Island, British Columbia

Tel: +1 604 233 0460
www.condenastjohansens.com/sonoraresort

CANADA - ONTARIO (NIAGARA-ON-THE-LAKE)

Harbour House

85 Melville Street, Box 760, Niagara-on-the-Lake,
Ontario L0S 1J0

Tel: +1 905 468 4683
www.condenastjohansens.com/harbourhouseca

CANADA - BRITISH COLUMBIA (SOOKE)

Sooke Harbour House

1528 Whiffen Spit Road, Sooke, British Columbia
V9Z 0T4

Tel: +1 250 642 3421
www.condenastjohansens.com/sookeharbour

CANADA - ONTARIO (TORONTO)

Windsor Arms

18 St. Thomas Street, Toronto, Ontario M5S 3E7

Tel: +1 416 971 9666
www.condenastjohansens.com/windsorarms

CANADA - BRITISH COLUMBIA (TOFINO)

Clayoquot Wilderness Resort

P.O. Box 130, Tofino, British Columbia V0R 2Z0

Tel: +1 250 726 8235
www.condenastjohansens.com/clayoquot

CANADA - QUÉBEC (MONT-TREMBLANT)

Hôtel Quintessence

3004 chemin de la chapelle, Mont-Tremblant, Québec
J8E 1E1

Tel: +1 819 425 3400
www.condenastjohansens.com/quintessence

CANADA - BRITISH COLUMBIA (TOFINO)

Wickaninnish Inn

Osprey Lane at Chesterman Beach, Tofino, British
Columbia V0R 2Z0

Tel: +1 250 725 3100
www.condenastjohansens.com/wickaninnish

CANADA - QUÉBEC (NORTH HATLEY)

Manoir Hovey

575 Hovey Road, North Hatley, Québec J0B 2C0

Tel: +1 819 842 2421
www.condenastjohansens.com/manoirhovey

CANADA - BRITISH COLUMBIA (VANCOUVER)

Loden Hotel

1177 Melville Street, Vancouver, British Columbia
V6E 0A3

Tel: +1 604 669 5060
www.condenastjohansens.com/theloden

MÉXICO - GUANAJUATO (GUANAJUATO)

Villa Maria Cristina

Paseo de La Presa de la Olla No. 76 Centro, Guanajuato,
Guanajuato 36000

Tel: +52 473 731 2182
www.condenastjohansens.com/villamariacristina

Hotels - The Americas

Properties listed below can be found in our Recommended Hotels, Inns, Resorts & Spas – The Americas, Atlantic, Caribbean & Pacific 2012 Guide

MÉXICO - GUERRERO (ACAPULCO)

Las Brisas Acapulco

Carretera Escenica 5255, Acapulco, Guerrero 39867

Tel: +52 744 469 6900
www.condenastjohansens.com/brisasacapulco

MÉXICO - MÉXICO (VALLE DE BRAVO)

Hotel Rodavento

Km.3.5 Carretera Valle de Bravo -Los Saucos, Valle de Bravo, MéxIco 51200

Tel: +52 726 251 4182
www.condenastjohansens.com/rodavento

MÉXICO - GUERRERO (IXTAPA - ZIHUATANEJO)

Loma del Mar

Ixtapa - Zihuatanejo, Guerrero 40884

Tel: +52 755 555 0460
www.condenastjohansens.com/lomadelmar

MÉXICO - MORELOS (CUERNAVACA)

Las Mañanitas Hotel, Garden Restaurant & Spa

Ricardo Linares 107, Centro 62000, Cuernavaca, Morelos

Tel: +52 777 362 00 00
www.condenastjohansens.com/lasmananitas

MÉXICO - JALISCO (COSTALEGRE - PUERTO VALLARTA)

Las Alamandas Resort

Carretera Barra de Navidad - Puerto Vallarta km 83.5, Col. Quemaro, Jalisco 48850

Tel: +52 322 285 5500
www.condenastjohansens.com/alamandas

MÉXICO - MORELOS (TEPOZTLÁN)

Hostal de La Luz

Carretera Federal Tepoztlán, Amatlan Km. 4, Tepoztlán, Morelos 62524

Tel: +1 739 393 3076
www.condenastjohansens.com/hostaldelaluz

MÉXICO - JALISCO (GUADALAJARA)

Del Carmen Concept Hotel

Jacobo Galvez No.45, Zona Centro, Guadalajara, Jalisco 44100

Tel: +52 33 3614 2640/9875
www.condenastjohansens.com/delcarmen

MÉXICO - NAYARIT (PUNTA DE MITA)

Casa Papelillos

Punta de Mita, Nayarit 63734

Tel: +1 214 924 6427
www.condenastjohansens.com/casapapelillos

MÉXICO - JALISCO (JOCOTEPEC)

El Chante Spa Hotel

Rivera del Lago 170-1, El Chante, Jocotepec, Jalisco 45825

Tel: +52 387 763 26 08
www.condenastjohansens.com/elchantespa

MÉXICO - NAYARIT (PUNTA DE MITA)

Imanta Resorts Punta de Mita, México

Montenahuac Lote-L, Higuera Blanca, Nayarit CP63734

Tel: +52 329 298 4200
www.condenastjohansens.com/imantaresorts

MÉXICO - JALISCO (PUERTO VALLARTA)

Casa Velas

Pelicanos 311, Fracc. Marina Vallarta, Puerto Vallarta, Jalisco 48354

Tel: +52 322 226 6688
www.condenastjohansens.com/casavelas

MÉXICO - OAXACA (HUATULCO)

Casa Bichu

Estacahuite Bay, Puerto Ángel, Oaxaca 70902

Tel: +52 958 58 434 89
www.condenastjohansens.com/casabichu

MÉXICO - JALISCO (PUERTO VALLARTA)

Garza Blanca Preserve Resort & Spa

Km. 7.5 Carretera a Barra de Navidad, Puerto Vallarta, Jalisco 48390

Tel: +52 322 176 0700
www.condenastjohansens.com/garzablancaresort

MÉXICO - QUINTANA ROO (CANCÚN - PUERTO MORELOS)

Ceiba del Mar Beach & Spa Resort

Costera Norte Lte. 1, S.M. 10, MZ. 26, Puerto Morelos, Quintana Roo 77580

Tel: +1 877 545 6221
www.condenastjohansens.com/ceibadelmar

MÉXICO - MÉXICO (NUEVO VALLARTA - RIVIERA NAYARIT)

Villa La Estancia Riviera Nayarit

Paseo Cocoteros 750 Sur, Condominio Maestro Flamingos, Nuevo Vallarta, Riviera Nayarit 63732

Tel: +52 322 226 9700
www.condenastjohansens.com/villalaestancia

MÉXICO - QUINTANA ROO (PLAYA DEL CARMEN)

Le Reve Hotel & Spa

Playa Xcalacoco Fraccion 2A, Playa del Carmen, Quintana Roo 77710

Tel: +52 984 109 5660/5661
www.condenastjohansens.com/hotellereve

Hotels - The Americas

Properties listed below can be found in our Recommended Hotels, Inns, Resorts & Spas – The Americas, Atlantic, Caribbean & Pacific 2012 Guide

MÉXICO - VERACRUZ (JALCOMULCO)

Rio y Montaña

Domicilio Conocido, Col. Centro, Jalcomulco,
Veracruz 9400

Tel: +52 279 8323 596
www.condenastjohansens.com/rioymontana

U.S.A. - CALIFORNIA (BIG SUR)

Post Ranch Inn

Highway 1, P.O. Box 219, Big Sur, California 93920

Tel: +1 831 667 2200
www.condenastjohansens.com/postranchinn

MÉXICO - YUCATÁN (MÉRIDA)

Hacienda Xcanatún - Casa de Piedra

Calle 20 S/N, Comisaría Xcanatún, Km. 12 Carretera
Mérida - Progreso, Mérida, Yucatán 97302

Tel: +52 999 930 2140
www.condenastjohansens.com/xcanatun

U.S.A. - CALIFORNIA (BIG SUR)

Ventana Inn and Spa

48123 Highway One, Big Sur, California 93920

Tel: +1 831 667 2331
www.condenastjohansens.com/ventanainn

U.S.A. - ARIZONA (GREER)

Hidden Meadow Ranch

620 County Road 1325, Greer, Arizona 85927

Tel: +1 928 333 1000
www.condenastjohansens.com/hiddenmeadow

U.S.A. - CALIFORNIA (CALISTOGA)

Cottage Grove Inn

1711 Lincoln Avenue, Calistoga, California 94515

Tel: +1 707 942 8400/2657
www.condenastjohansens.com/cottagegrove

U.S.A. - ARIZONA (PARADISE VALLEY)

The Hermosa Inn

5532 North Palo Cristi Road, Paradise Valley,
Arizona 85253

Tel: +1 602 955 8614
www.condenastjohansens.com/hermosa

U.S.A. - CALIFORNIA (CARMEL-BY-THE-SEA)

L'Auberge Carmel

Monte Verde at Seventh, Carmel-by-the-Sea,
California 93921

Tel: +1 831 624 8578
www.condenastjohansens.com/laubergecarmel

U.S.A. - ARIZONA (PARADISE VALLEY - SCOTTSDALE)

Sanctuary on Camelback Mountain

5700 East McDonald Drive, Scottsdale, Arizona 85253

Tel: +1 480 948 2100
www.condenastjohansens.com/sanctuaryaz

U.S.A. - CALIFORNIA (CARMEL-BY-THE-SEA)

Tradewinds Carmel

Mission Street at Third Avenue, Carmel-by-the-Sea,
California 93921

Tel: +1 831 624 2776
www.condenastjohansens.com/tradewinds

U.S.A. - ARIZONA (TUCSON)

Hacienda del Sol Guest Ranch Resort

5501 N. Hacienda del Sol Road, Tucson, Arizona 85718

Tel: +1 520 299 1501
www.condenastjohansens.com/haciendadelsol

U.S.A. - CALIFORNIA (CARMEL VALLEY)

Bernardus Lodge

415 Carmel Valley Road, Carmel Valley, California 93924

Tel: +1 831 658 3400
www.condenastjohansens.com/bernardus

U.S.A. - ARIZONA (TUCSON)

Tanque Verde Ranch

14301 East Speedway Boulevard, Tucson,
Arizona 85748

Tel: +1 520 296 6275
www.condenastjohansens.com/tanqueverde

U.S.A. - CALIFORNIA (HEALDSBURG)

Hotel Les Mars

27 North Street, Healdsburg, California 95448

Tel: +1 707 433 4211
www.condenastjohansens.com/lesmarshotel

U.S.A. - ARIZONA (TUCSON)

Westward Look Resort

245 E. Ina Road, Tuscon, Arizona 85704

Tel: +1 520 297 1151
www.condenastjohansens.com/westwardlook

U.S.A. - CALIFORNIA (LA JOLLA)

Grande Colonial Hotel La Jolla

910 Prospect Street, La Jolla, California 92037

Tel: +1 855 380 4454
www.condenastjohansens.com/gclj

Hotels - The Americas

Properties listed below can be found in our Recommended Hotels, Inns, Resorts & Spas – The Americas, Atlantic, Caribbean & Pacific 2012 Guide

U.S.A. - CALIFORNIA (LA JOLLA)
Hotel Parisi

1111 Prospect Street, La Jolla, California 92037

Tel: +1 858 454 1511
www.condenastjohansens.com/hotelparisi

U.S.A. - CALIFORNIA (SAN FRANCISCO BAY AREA)
Inn Above Tide

30 El Portal, Sausalito, California 94965

Tel: +1 415 332 9535
www.condenastjohansens.com/innabovetide

U.S.A. - CALIFORNIA (LAKE TAHOE)
PlumpJack Squaw Valley Inn

1920 Squaw Valley Road, Olympic Valley,
California 96146

Tel: +1 530 583 1576
www.condenastjohansens.com/plumpjack

U.S.A. - CALIFORNIA (YOUNTVILLE)
Bardessono

6526 Yount Street, Yountville, California 94599

Tel: +1 707 204 6000
www.condenastjohansens.com/bardessono

U.S.A. - CALIFORNIA (MENDOCINO)
The Stanford Inn By The Sea

Coast Highway One & Comptche-Ukiah Road,
Mendocino, California 95460

Tel: +1 707 937 5615
www.condenastjohansens.com/stanfordinn

U.S.A. - COLORADO (DENVER)
Castle Marne Bed & Breakfast Inn

1572 Race Street, Denver, Colorado 80206

Tel: +1 303 331 0621
www.condenastjohansens.com/castlemarne

U.S.A. - CALIFORNIA (MONTEREY)
Old Monterey Inn

500 Martin Street, Monterey, California 93940

Tel: +1 831 375 8284
www.condenastjohansens.com/oldmontereyinn

U.S.A. - COLORADO (ESTES PARK)
Taharaa Mountain Lodge

P.O. Box 2586, 3110 So. St. Vrain, Estes Park,
Colorado 80517

Tel: +1 970 577 0098
www.condenastjohansens.com/taharaa

U.S.A. - CALIFORNIA (NAPA)
1801 First Inn

1801 First Street, Napa, California 94559

Tel: +1 707 224 3739
www.condenastjohansens.com/1801first

U.S.A. - COLORADO (STEAMBOAT SPRINGS)
Vista Verde Guest Ranch

P.O. Box 770465, Steamboat Springs, Colorado 80477

Tel: +1 970 879 3858
www.condenastjohansens.com/vistaverderanch

U.S.A. - CALIFORNIA (NAPA)
Milliken Creek Inn & Spa

1815 Silverado Trail, Napa, California 94558

Tel: +1 707 255 1197
www.condenastjohansens.com/milliken

U.S.A. - COLORADO (TELLURIDE)
Hotel Columbia

301 West San Juan Avenue, Telluride, Colorado 81435

Tel: +1 970 728 0660/6294
www.condenastjohansens.com/columbiatelluride

U.S.A. - CALIFORNIA (NAPA)
White House Inn & Spa

443 Brown Street, Napa, California 94559

Tel: +1 707 254 9301
www.condenastjohansens.com/whitehousenapa

U.S.A. - COLORADO (TELLURIDE)
lumiére Telluride

118 Lost Creek Lane, Telluride, Colorado 81435

Tel: +1 970 369 0400
www.condenastjohansens.com/lumiere

U.S.A. - CALIFORNIA (RANCHO SANTA FE)
The Inn at Rancho Santa Fe

5951 Linea del Cielo, Rancho Santa Fe, California 92067

Tel: +1 858 756 1131
www.condenastjohansens.com/ranchosantafe

U.S.A. - COLORADO (VAIL)
The Sebastian - Vail

16 Vail Road, Vail, Colorado 81657

Tel: +1 970 331 0655
www.condenastjohansens.com/thesebastianvail

Properties listed below can be found in our Recommended Hotels, Inns, Resorts & Spas – The Americas, Atlantic, Caribbean & Pacific 2012 Guide

U.S.A. - COLORADO (VAIL)

Vail Mountain Lodge & Spa

352 East Meadow Drive, Vail, Colorado 81657

Tel: +1 970 476 0700
www.condenastjohansens.com/vailmountain

U.S.A. - FLORIDA (MIAMI BEACH)

The Setai South Beach

2001 Collins Avenue, Miami Beach, Florida 33139

Tel: +1 305 520 6000/6110
www.condenastjohansens.com/setai

U.S.A. - DELAWARE (REHOBOTH BEACH)

Boardwalk Plaza Hotel

Olive Avenue & The Boardwalk, Rehoboth Beach, Delaware 19971

Tel: +1 302 227 7169
www.condenastjohansens.com/boardwalkplaza

U.S.A. - GEORGIA (CUMBERLAND ISLAND)

Greyfield Inn

Cumberland Island, Georgia

Tel: +1 904 261 6408
www.condenastjohansens.com/greyfieldinn

U.S.A. - DELAWARE (WILMINGTON)

Inn at Montchanin Village & Spa

Route 100 & Kirk Road, Montchanin, Wilmington, Delaware 19710

Tel: +1 302 888 2133
www.condenastjohansens.com/montchanin

U.S.A. - ILLINOIS (CHICAGO)

Trump International Hotel & Tower® Chicago

401 North Wabash Avenue, Chicago, Illinois 60611

Tel: +1 312 588 8000
www.condenastjohansens.com/trumpchicago

U.S.A. - DISTRICT OF COLUMBIA (WASHINGTON D.C.)

The Hay-Adams

Sixteenth & H. Streets N.W., Washington D.C., District of Columbia 20006

Tel: +1 202 638 6600
www.condenastjohansens.com/hayadams

U.S.A. - MAINE (CAMDEN)

Camden Harbour Inn

83 Bayview Street, Camden, Maine 04843

Tel: +1 207 236 4200
www.condenastjohansens.com/camdenharbourinn

U.S.A. - FLORIDA (BAL HARBOUR, MIAMI BEACH)

ONE Bal Harbour

10295 Collins Avenue, Bal Harbour, Florida 33154

Tel: +1 305 455 5400/5459
www.condenastjohansens.com/onebalharbour

U.S.A. - MAINE (KENNEBUNK BEACH)

The White Barn Inn & Spa

37 Beach Avenue, Kennebunk Beach, Maine 04043

Tel: +1 207 967 2321
www.condenastjohansens.com/whitebarninn

U.S.A. - FLORIDA (FISHER ISLAND)

Fisher Island Club & Resort

One Fisher Island Drive, Fisher Island, Florida 33109

Tel: +1 305 535 6000
www.condenastjohansens.com/fisherisland

U.S.A. - MAINE (PORTLAND)

Portland Harbor Hotel

468 Fore Street, Portland, Maine 04101

Tel: +1 207 775 9090
www.condenastjohansens.com/portlandharbor

U.S.A. - FLORIDA (FORT LAUDERDALE)

The Pillars Hotel

111 North Birch Road, Fort Lauderdale, Florida 33304

Tel: +1 954 467 9639
www.condenastjohansens.com/pillarshotel

U.S.A. - MASSACHUSETTS (BOSTON)

Boston Harbor Hotel

70 Rowes Wharf, Boston, Massachusetts 02110

Tel: +1 617 439 7000
www.condenastjohansens.com/bhh

U.S.A. - FLORIDA (MIAMI BEACH)

The Betsy

1440 Ocean Drive, Miami Beach, Florida 33139

Tel: +1 305 531 6100
www.condenastjohansens.com/thebetsyhotel

U.S.A. - MASSACHUSETTS (BOSTON)

Fifteen Beacon

15 Beacon Street, Boston, Massachusetts 02108

Tel: +1 617 670 1500
www.condenastjohansens.com/xvbeacon

Hotels - The Americas

Properties listed below can be found in our Recommended Hotels, Inns, Resorts & Spas – The Americas, Atlantic, Caribbean & Pacific 2012 Guide

U.S.A. - MASSACHUSETTS (BOSTON)

Hotel Commonwealth

500 Commonwealth Avenue, Boston,
Massachusetts 02215

Tel: +1 617 933 5000
www.condenastjohansens.com/commonwealth

U.S.A. - NEW YORK (NEW YORK CITY)

Hôtel Plaza Athénée

37 East 64th Street, New York City, New York 10065

Tel: +1 212 734 9100
www.condenastjohansens.com/athenee

U.S.A. - MASSACHUSETTS (CAMBRIDGE)

The Hotel Veritas

One Remington Street in Harvard Square, Cambridge,
Massachusetts 02138

Tel: +1 617 520 5000
www.condenastjohansens.com/thehotelveritas

U.S.A. - NEW YORK (NEW YORK CITY)

The Inn at Irving Place

56 Irving Place, New York, New York City 10003

Tel: +1 212 533 4600
www.condenastjohansens.com/irving

U.S.A. - MASSACHUSETTS (IPSWICH)

The Inn at Castle Hill

280 Argilla Road, Ipswich, Massachusetts 01938

Tel: +1 978 412 2555
www.condenastjohansens.com/castlehill

U.S.A. - NEW YORK (NEW YORK CITY)

The Mark

Madison Avenue at East 77th Street, New York City,
New York 10075

Tel: +1 212 744 4300
www.condenastjohansens.com/themark

U.S.A. - MASSACHUSETTS (LENOX)

Blantyre

16 Blantyre Road, P.O. Box 995, Lenox,
Massachusetts 01240

Tel: +1 413 637 3556
www.condenastjohansens.com/blantyre

U.S.A. - NEW YORK (VERONA)

The Lodge at Turning Stone

5218 Patrick Road, Verona, New York 13478

Tel: +1 315 361 8525
www.condenastjohansens.com/turningstone

U.S.A. - MASSACHUSETTS (MARTHA'S VINEYARD)

The Charlotte Inn

27 South Summer Street, Edgartown, Massachusetts
02539

Tel: +1 508 627 4751/4151
www.condenastjohansens.com/charlotte

U.S.A. - NEW YORK/LONG ISLAND (EAST HAMPTON)

The Baker House 1650

181 Main Street, East Hampton, New York 11937

Tel: +1 631 324 4081
www.condenastjohansens.com/bakerhouse

U.S.A. - MONTANA (DARBY)

Triple Creek Ranch

5551 West Fork Road, Darby, Montana 59829

Tel: +1 406 821 4600
www.condenastjohansens.com/triplecreek

U.S.A. - NEW YORK/LONG ISLAND (SOUTHAMPTON)

1708 House

126 Main Street, Southampton, New York 11968

Tel: +1 631 287 1708
www.condenastjohansens.com/1708house

U.S.A. - NEVADA (LAS VEGAS)

SKYLOFTS at MGM Grand

3977 Las Vegas Boulevard South, Las Vegas,
Nevada 89109

Tel: +1 702 891 3832
www.condenastjohansens.com/skylofts

U.S.A. - NORTH CAROLINA (HIGHLANDS)

Inn at Half Mile Farm

P.O. Box 2769, 214 Half Mile Drive, Highlands,
North Carolina 28741

Tel: +1 828 526 8170
www.condenastjohansens.com/halfmilefarm

U.S.A. - NEW MEXICO (ALBUQUERQUE)

Los Poblanos Inn & Organic Farm

4803 Rio Grande Blvd NW, Los Ranchos de
Albuquerque, New Mexico 87107

Tel: +505 344 9297
www.condenastjohansens.com/lospoblanos

U.S.A. - NORTH CAROLINA (SOUTHERN PINES)

The Jefferson Inn

150 West New Hampshire Avenue, Southern Pines,
North Carolina 28387

Tel: +1 910 692 9911
www.condenastjohansens.com/jeffersoninn

Properties listed below can be found in our Recommended Hotels, Inns, Resorts & Spas – The Americas, Atlantic, Caribbean & Pacific 2012 Guide

U.S.A. - RHODE ISLAND (NEWPORT)

Castle Hill Inn

590 Ocean Drive, Newport, Rhode Island 02840

Tel: +1 401 849 3800
www.condenastjohansens.com/castlehillinn

U.S.A. - WASHINGTON (SPOKANE)

Hotel Lusso

808 West Sprague Avenue, Spokane, Washington 99201

Tel: +1 509 747 9750
www.condenastjohansens.com/hotellusso

U.S.A. - RHODE ISLAND (NEWPORT)

Vanderbilt Grace

41 Mary Street, Newport, Rhode Island 02840

Tel: +1 401 846 6200
www.condenastjohansens.com/vanderbiltgrace

U.S.A. - WYOMING (JACKSON HOLE)

Amangani

1535 North East Butte Road, P.O. Box 15030, Jackson Hole, Wyoming 83002

Tel: +1 307 734 7333
www.condenastjohansens.com/amangani

U.S.A. - SOUTH CAROLINA (CHARLESTON)

Charleston Harbor Resort & Marina

20 Patriots Point Road, Charleston, South Carolina 29464

Tel: +1 843 856 0028
www.condenastjohansens.com/charlestonharbor

U.S.A. - WYOMING (SARATOGA)

The Lodge and Spa at Brush Creek Ranch

66 Brush Creek Ranch Road, Saratoga, Wyoming 82331

Tel: +1 307 327 5284
www.condenastjohansens.com/brushcreekranch

U.S.A. - VERMONT (WEST TOWNSHEND)

Windham Hill Inn

311 Lawrence Drive, West Townshend, Vermont 05359

Tel: +1 802 874 4080
www.condenastjohansens.com/windhamhillinn

BELIZE - AMBERGRIS CAYE (CAYO ESPANTO)

Cayo Espanto a private island

Ambergris Caye, Cayo Espanto

Tel: +910 323 8355
www.condenastjohansens.com/cayoespanto

U.S.A. - VIRGINIA (MIDDLEBURG)

The Goodstone Inn & Estate

36205 Snake Hill Road, Middleburg, Virginia 20117

Tel: +1 540 687 4645
www.condenastjohansens.com/goodstoneinn

BELIZE - AMBERGRIS CAYE (SAN PEDRO)

Belizean Cove Estates

P.O. Box 1, San Pedro, Ambergris Caye

Tel: +501 226 4741
www.condenastjohansens.com/belizeancove

U.S.A. - VIRGINIA (RICHMOND)

The Jefferson

101 West Franklin Street, Richmond, Virginia 23220

Tel: +1 804 788 8000
www.condenastjohansens.com/jeffersonva

BELIZE - AMBERGRIS CAYE (SAN PEDRO)

Coco Beach Resort

P.O. Box 1, San Pedro, Ambergris Caye

Tel: +501 226 4741
www.condenastjohansens.com/cocobeachbelize

U.S.A. - WASHINGTON (BELLEVUE)

Hotel Bellevue

11200 S.E. 6th Street, Bellevue, Washington 98004

Tel: +1 425 454 4424
www.condenastjohansens.com/bellevue

BELIZE - AMBERGRIS CAYE (NEAR SAN PEDRO)

Matachica Resort & Spa

5 miles North of San Pedro, Ambergris Caye

Tel: +501 226 5010
www.condenastjohansens.com/matachica

U.S.A. - WASHINGTON (SPOKANE)

The Davenport Hotel and Tower

10 South Post Street, Spokane, Washington 99201

Tel: +1 509 455 8888
www.condenastjohansens.com/davenport

BELIZE - AMBERGRIS CAYE (SAN PEDRO)

Victoria House

P.O. Box 22, San Pedro, Ambergris Caye

Tel: +501 226 2067
www.condenastjohansens.com/victoriahouse

Hotels - The Americas

Properties listed below can be found in our Recommended Hotels, Inns, Resorts & Spas – The Americas, Atlantic, Caribbean & Pacific 2012 Guide

BELIZE - CAYO DISTRICT (MOUNTAIN PINE RIDGE FOREST RESERVE)

Blancaneaux Lodge

Mountain Pine Ridge Forest Reserve, Cayo District

Tel: +501 824 4912/4914
www.condenastjohansens.com/blancaneaux

BELIZE - CAYO DISTRICT (MOUNTAIN PINE RIDGE FOREST RESERVE)

Hidden Valley Inn

P.O. Box 170, Belmopan

Tel: +501 822 3320
www.condenastjohansens.com/hiddenvalleyinn

BELIZE - CAYO DISTRICT (SAN IGNACIO)

The Lodge at Chaa Creek

P.O. Box 53, San Ignacio, Cayo District

Tel: +501 824 2037
www.condenastjohansens.com/chaacreek

BELIZE - ORANGE WALK DISTRICT (GALLON JUG ESTATE)

Chan Chich Lodge

Gallon Jug Estate, Orange Walk District

Tel: +501 223 4419
www.condenastjohansens.com/chanchich

BELIZE - STANN CREEK DISTRICT (PLACENCIA VILLAGE)

Turtle Inn

Placencia Village, Stann Creek District

Tel: +501 824 4912/4914
www.condenastjohansens.com/turtleinn

BELIZE - TOLEDO DISTRICT (PUNTA GORDA)

Machaca Hill Rainforest Canopy Lodge

P.O. Box 135, Punta Gorda, Toledo District

Tel: +501 722 0050
www.condenastjohansens.com/machacahill

COSTA RICA - ALAJUELA (LA FORTUNA DE SAN CARLOS)

Nayara Hotel, Spa & Gardens

600 Metros Noreste, La Fortuna de San Carlos, Arenal Volcano National Park 33021

Tel: +506 2479 1600
www.condenastjohansens.com/arenalnayara

COSTA RICA - ALAJUELA (LA FORTUNA DE SAN CARLOS)

Tabacón Grand Spa Thermal Resort

La Fortuna de San Carlos, Arenal

Tel: +506 2519 1900
www.condenastjohansens.com/tabacon

COSTA RICA - GUANACASTE (NICOYA)

Hotel Punta Islita

Islita, Nicoya, Guanacaste

Tel: +506 2656 3036
www.condenastjohansens.com/hotelpuntaislita

COSTA RICA - GUANACASTE (PINILLA)

La Posada Hotel

Hacienda Pinilla, Pinilla, Guanacaste

Tel: +506 2680 3000
www.condenastjohansens.com/laposadapinilla

COSTA RICA - LIMÓN (PUERTO VIEJO)

Le Caméléon

Cocles Beach, Puerto Viejo, Limón

Tel: +506 2291 7750
www.condenastjohansens.com/lecameleon

COSTA RICA - PUNTARENAS (MANUEL ANTONIO)

Gaia Hotel & Reserve

Km 2.7 Carretera Quepos, Manuel Antonio, Puntarenas

Tel: +506 2777 9797
www.condenastjohansens.com/gaiahr

COSTA RICA - PUNTARENAS (MANUEL ANTONIO)

The Suu Manuel Antonio

Carretera a Punta Quepos, Manuel Antonio, Puntarenas

Tel: +506 2777 7373
www.condenastjohansens.com/manuelantonio

COSTA RICA - PUNTARENAS (PLAYA DOMINICAL)

Villa Paraiso

Playa Dominical, Puntarenas

Tel: +506 2787 0258
www.condenastjohansens.com/villaparaiso

COSTA RICA - PUNTARENAS (SANTA TERESA)

Florblanca

Santa Teresa, Puntarenas

Tel: +506 2640 0232
www.condenastjohansens.com/florblanca

GUATEMALA - SACATEPÉQUEZ (LA ANTIGUA GUATEMALA)

Casa Quinta Hotel Boutique

5 Av. Sur No. 45, La Antigua Guatemala, Sacatepéquez

Tel: +502 7832 6181/6083
www.condenastjohansens.com/hotelcasaquinta

Properties listed below can be found in our Recommended Hotels, Inns, Resorts & Spas – The Americas, Atlantic, Caribbean & Pacific 2012 Guide

GUATEMALA - SACATEPÉQUEZ (LA ANTIGUA GUATEMALA)

El Convento Boutique Hotel Antigua Guatemala

2a Avenue Norte 11, La Antigua Guatemala, Sacatepéquez

Tel: +502 7720 7272

www.condenastjohansens.com/elconventoantigua

GUATEMALA - SACATEPÉQUEZ (LA ANTIGUA GUATEMALA)

Palacio de Doña Leonor Antigua Guatemala

4a Calle Oriente Casa No. 8, La Antigua Guatemala, Sacatepéquez 03001

Tel: +502 7832 2281

www.condenastjohansens.com/palaciodeleonor

GUATEMALA - SACATEPÉQUEZ (SAN JUAN ALOTENANGO - LA ANTIGUA GUATEMALA)

La Reunión Antigua Golf Resort

Km. 91.5 Ruta Nacional 14, San Juan Alotenango, Sacatepéquez

Tel: +502 7873 1400

www.condenastjohansens.com/lareunion

GUATEMALA - SOLOLÁ (LAKE ATITLÁN)

Hotel Atitlán

Finca San Buenaventura, Panajachel, Lake Atitlán, Sololá 07010

Tel: +502 7762 1441/2060

www.condenastjohansens.com/hotelatitlan

HONDURAS - BAY ISLANDS (ROATÁN)

Mayoka Lodge

Sandy Bay, Roatán, Bay Islands

Tel: +504 2445 3043

www.condenastjohansens.com/mayokalodge

ARGENTINA - BUENOS AIRES (CIUDAD DE BUENOS AIRES)

Duque Hotel Boutique & Spa

Guatemala 4364, Ciudad de Buenos Aires, Buenos Aires

Tel: +54 11 4832 0312

www.condenastjohansens.com/duquehotel

ARGENTINA - BUENOS AIRES (CIUDAD DE BUENOS AIRES)

Fierro Hotel

Soler 5862, Palermo Hollywood, C1425BYK Ciudad de Buenos Aires, Buenos Aires

Tel: +54 11 3220 6800

www.condenastjohansens.com/fierrohotel

ARGENTINA - BUENOS AIRES (CIUDAD DE BUENOS AIRES)

Legado Mitico

Gurruchaga 1848, C1414DIL Ciudad de Buenos Aires, Buenos Aires

Tel: +54 11 4833 1300

www.condenastjohansens.com/legadomitico

ARGENTINA - BUENOS AIRES (CIUDAD DE BUENOS AIRES)

Mine Hotel Boutique

Gorriti 4770, Palermo Soho, C1414BJL Ciudad de Buenos Aires, Buenos Aires

Tel: +54 11 4832 1100

www.condenastjohansens.com/minehotel

ARGENTINA - RÍO NEGRO (PATAGONIA - SAN CARLOS DE BARILOCHE)

Llao Llao Hotel & Resort, Golf-Spa

Av. Ezequiel Bustillo Km 25, San Carlos de Bariloche, Río Negro, Patagonia

Tel: +54 2944 44 8530

www.condenastjohansens.com/llaollao

BRAZIL - ALAGOAS (BARRA DE SÃO MIGUEL)

Kenoa - Exclusive Beach Spa & Resort

Rua Escritor Jorge Lima 58, Barra de São Miguel, Alagoas 57180-000

Tel: +55 82 3272 1285

www.condenastjohansens.com/kenoaresort

BRAZIL - ALAGOAS (PORTO DE PEDRAS)

Pousada Patacho

Praia do Patacho s/n, Porto de Pedras, Alagoas 57945-000

Tel: +55 82 3298 1253

www.condenastjohansens.com/pousadapatacho

BRAZIL - ALAGOAS (SÃO MIGUEL DOS MILAGRES)

Pousada do Toque

Rua Felisberto de Ataide, Povoado do Toque, São Miguel dos Milagres, Alagoas 57940-000

Tel: +55 82 3295 1127

www.condenastjohansens.com/pousadadotoque

BRAZIL - BAHIA (ARRAIAL D'AJUDA)

Maitei Hotel

Estrada do Mucugê 475, Arraial D'Ajuda, Porto Seguro, Bahia 45816-000

Tel: +55 73 3575 3877/3799

www.condenastjohansens.com/maitei

BRAZIL - BAHIA (CORUMBAU)

Fazenda São Francisco

Ponta do Corumbau, Bahia

Tel: +55 11 3078 4411

www.condenastjohansens.com/fazenda

BRAZIL - BAHIA (CORUMBAU)

Vila Naiá - Paralelo 17°

Ponta do Corumbau, Bahia

Tel: +55 11 3061 1872

www.condenastjohansens.com/vilanaia

Hotels - The Americas

Properties listed below can be found in our Recommended Hotels, Inns, Resorts & Spas – The Americas, Atlantic, Caribbean & Pacific 2012 Guide

BRAZIL - BAHIA (ITACARÉ)

Txai Resort

Rod. Ilhéus-Itacaré km. 48, Itacaré, Bahia 45530-000

Tel: +55 73 2101 5000
www.condenastjohansens.com/txairesort

BRAZIL - PERNAMBUCO (FERNANDO DE NORONHA)

Pousada Maravilha

Rodovia BR-363, s/n, Sueste, Ilha de Fernando de Noronha, Pernambuco 53990-000

Tel: +55 81 3619 0028/1290/0163
www.condenastjohansens.com/maravilha

BRAZIL - BAHIA (PENÍNSULA DE MARAÚ - MARAÚ)

Kiaroa Eco-Luxury Resort

Loteamento da Costa, área SD6, Distrito de Barra Grande, Municipio de Maraú, Bahia, CEP 45 520-000

Tel: +55 73 3258 6214
www.condenastjohansens.com/kiaroa

BRAZIL - PERNAMBUCO (PORTO DE GALINHAS)

Nannai Beach Resort

Rodovia PE-09, acesso à Muro Alto, Km 3, Ipojuca, Pernambuco 55590-000

Tel: +55 81 3552 0100
www.condenastjohansens.com/nannaibeach

BRAZIL - BAHIA (TRANCOSO)

Etnia Pousada and Boutique

Trancoso, Bahia 45818-000

Tel: + 55 73 3668 1137
www.condenastjohansens.com/etnia

BRAZIL - RIO DE JANEIRO (ARMAÇÃO DOS BÚZIOS)

Villa Rasa Marina

Av. José Bento Ribeiro Dantas 299, Armação dos Búzios, Rio de Janeiro 28950-000

Tel: +55 22 2623 8345
www.condenastjohansens.com/villarasamarina

BRAZIL - BAHIA (TRANCOSO)

Uxua Casa Hotel

Praça São João, Quadrado, Trancoso, Porto Seguro, Bahia 45818-000

Tel: +55 73 3668 2277/2166
www.condenastjohansens.com/uxua

BRAZIL - RIO DE JANEIRO (BÚZIOS)

Casas Brancas Boutique-Hotel & Spa

Alto do Humaitá 10, Armação dos Búzios, Rio de Janeiro 28950-000

Tel: +55 22 2623 1458/1603
www.condenastjohansens.com/casasbrancas

BRAZIL - CEARÁ (JERICOACOARA)

Vila Kalango

Rua das Dunas 30, Jericoacoara, Ceará 62598-000

Tel: +55 88 3669 2290/2289
www.condenastjohansens.com/vilakalango

BRAZIL - RIO DE JANEIRO (BÚZIOS)

Hotel Le Relais La Borie

1374 Rua dos Gravatás, Praia de Geribá, Armação dos Búzios, Rio de Janeiro 28950-000

Tel: +55 22 2620 8504
www.condenastjohansens.com/laborie

BRAZIL - MINAS GERAIS (LIMA DUARTE)

Reserva do Ibitipoca

Fazenda do Engenho, s/n Conceição do Ibitipoca, Lima Duarte, Minas Gerais 36140-000

Tel: +55 32 3281 8174
www.condenastjohansens.com/reservadoibitipoca

BRAZIL - RIO DE JANEIRO (BÚZIOS)

Insólito Boutique Hotel

Rua E1 - Lotes 3 and 4 , Condomínio Atlântico, Armação de Búzios, Rio de Janeiro 28.950-000

Tel: +55 22 2623 2172
www.condenastjohansens.com/insolitohotel

BRAZIL - MINAS GERAIS (TIRADENTES)

Solar da Ponte

Praça das Mercês S/N, Tiradentes, Minas Gerais 36325-000

Tel: +55 32 33 55 12 55
www.condenastjohansens.com/solardaponte

BRAZIL - RIO DE JANEIRO (PARATY)

Casa Turquesa

50 rua Doutor Pereira, Centro Histórico Paraty, Rio de Janeiro

Tel: +55 24 3371 1037/1125
www.condenastjohansens.com/casaturquesa

BRAZIL - PARANÁ (FOZ DO IGUAÇU)

Hotel das Cataratas

Rodovia BR. 469 KM. 32, Iguassu National Park, Foz do Iguaçu, Paraná 85853-000

Tel: +55 45 2102 7000
www.condenastjohansens.com/hoteldascataratas

BRAZIL - RIO DE JANEIRO (PETRÓPOLIS)

Solar do Império

Koeler Avenue, 376 Centro, Petrópolis, Rio de Janeiro

Tel: +55 24 2103 3000
www.condenastjohansens.com/solardoimperio

Properties listed below can be found in our Recommended Hotels, Inns, Resorts & Spas – The Americas, Atlantic, Caribbean & Pacific 2012 Guide

BRAZIL - RIO DE JANEIRO (PETRÓPOLIS)

Tankamana EcoResort

Estrada Júlio Cápua, S/N Vale Do Cuiabá, Itaipava -
Petrópolis, Rio De Janeiro 25745-050

Tel: +55 24 2232 2900
www.condenastjohansens.com/tankamana

BRAZIL - RIO DE JANEIRO (RIO DE JANEIRO)

Hotel Marina All Suites

Av. Delfim Moreira, 696, Praia do Leblon,
Rio de Janeiro 22441-000

Tel: +55 21 2172 1001
www.condenastjohansens.com/marinaallsuites

BRAZIL - RIO GRANDE DO NORTE (PRAIA DA PIPA)

Toca da Coruja

Avenida Baia dos Golfinhos, 464, Praia da Pipa, Tibau
do Sul, Rio Grande do Norte 59178-000

Tel: +55 84 3246 2226/2225/2121
www.condenastjohansens.com/tocadacoruja

BRAZIL - RIO GRANDE DO SUL (GRAMADO)

Estalagem St. Hubertus

Rua Carrieri, 974, Gramado,
Rio Grande do Sul 95670-000

Tel: +55 54 3286 1273
www.condenastjohansens.com/sthubertus

BRAZIL - RIO GRANDE DO SUL (GRAMADO)

Kurotel Medical Longevity Center and Spa

Rua Nações Unidas 533, P.O. Box 65, Gramado,
Rio Grande do Sul 95670-000

Tel: +55 54 3295 9393
www.condenastjohansens.com/kurotel

BRAZIL - RIO GRANDE DO SUL (GRAMADO)

La Hacienda Inn and Restaurant

Estrada da Serra Grande 4200, Gramado, Rio Grande
do Sul 95670-000

Tel: +55 54 3295 3025/3088
www.condenastjohansens.com/lahacienda

BRAZIL - RIO GRANDE DO SUL (GRAMADO)

Varanda das Bromélias Boutique Hotel

Rua Alarich Schulz, 198 Bairro Planalto, 95670-000
Gramado, Rio Grande do Sul

Tel: +55 54 3286 0547
www.condenastjohansens.com/varandadasbromelias

BRAZIL - SANTA CATARINA (GOVERNADOR CELSO RAMOS)

Ponta dos Ganchos

Rua Eupídio Alves do Nascimento, 104, Governador
Celso Ramos, Santa Catarina 88190-000

Tel: +55 48 3953 7000
www.condenastjohansens.com/pontadosganchos

BRAZIL - SANTA CATARINA (PRAIA DO ROSA)

Pousada Solar Mirador

Estrada Geral do Rosa s/n, Praia do Rosa, Imbituba,
Santa Catarina 88780-000

Tel: +55 48 3355 6144/6004/6697
www.condenastjohansens.com/solarmirador

BRAZIL - SÃO PAULO (CAMPOS DO JORDÃO)

Hotel Frontenac

Av. Dr. Paulo Ribas, 295 Capivari, Campos do Jordão -
São Paulo 12460-000

Tel: +55 12 3669 1000
www.condenastjohansens.com/frontenac

BRAZIL - SÃO PAULO (ILHABELA)

DPNY Beach Hotel

Av. José Pacheco do Nascimento, 7668, Praia do Curral,
Ilhabela, São Paulo 11630-000

Tel: +55 12 3894 3000
www.condenastjohansens.com/dpnybeach

BRAZIL - SÃO PAULO (SANTO ANTÔNIO DO PINHAL)

Pousada Quinta dos Pinhais

Estrada do Pico Agudo, KM. 3, Santo Antônio do Pinhal,
São Paulo 12450-000

Tel: +55 12 3666 2030/2463/1731
www.condenastjohansens.com/quintadospinhais

BRAZIL - SÃO PAULO (SÃO PAULO)

Hotel Unique

Avenida Brigadeiro Luis Antonio, 4.700 São Paulo,
São Paulo 01402-002

Tel: +55 11 3055 4710/4700
www.condenastjohansens.com/hotelunique

BRAZIL - SÃO PAULO (SERRA DA CANTAREIRA)

Spa Unique Garden

Estrada Laramara, 3500, Serra da Cantareira,
São Paulo 07600-970

Tel: +55 11 4486 8700
www.condenastjohansens.com/uniquegarden

CHILE - IX REGIÓN DE ARAUCANÍA (VILLARRICA/PUCÓN)

**Villarrica Park Lake, a Luxury Collection
Hotel & Spa**

Camino Villarrica - Pucón Km 13, Villarrica,
IX Región de Araucanía

Tel: +56 45 45 00 00
www.condenastjohansens.com/villarrica

CHILE - X REGIÓN DE LOS LAGOS (PATAGONIA - PUERTO
MONTT)

Nomads of the Seas

Puerto Montt, X Región de los Lagos

Tel: +562 414 4600
www.condenastjohansens.com/nomadsoftheseas

Hotels - The Americas

Properties listed below can be found in our Recommended Hotels, Inns, Resorts & Spas – The Americas, Atlantic, Caribbean & Pacific 2012 Guide

COLOMBIA - BOGOTÁ (SANTAFE DE BOGOTÁ)

Hotel 101 Park House Suites & Spa

Carrera 21 No. 101-10, Santafe de Bogotá, Bogotá

Tel: +57 1 600 0101

www.condenastjohansens.com/101parkhouse

ECUADOR - GALÁPAGOS ISLANDS (SANTA CRUZ ISLAND)

Royal Palm Hotel - Galápagos

Km. 18 Via Baltra, Santa Cruz Island, Galápagos Islands

Tel: +593 5 252 7408

www.condenastjohansens.com/royalpalmgalapagos

COLOMBIA - BOLÍVAR (CARTAGENA DE INDIAS)

Anandá Hotel Boutique

Calle del Cuartel N. 36-77, Cartagena de Indias, Bolívar

Tel: +57 5 664 4452

www.condenastjohansens.com/anandacartagena

ECUADOR - IMBABURA (ANGOCHAGUA)

Hacienda Zuleta

Angochagua, Imbabura

Tel: +593 6 266 2182

www.condenastjohansens.com/zuleta

COLOMBIA - BOLÍVAR (CARTAGENA DE INDIAS)

Casa Pestagua

Calle Santo Domingo No. 33-63, Cartagena de Indias, Bolívar

Tel: +57 5 664 9510/6286

www.condenastjohansens.com/casapestagua

ECUADOR - IMBABURA (SAN PABLO DEL LAGO)

4 Volcanoes Lodge

Calle Sucre, San Pablo del Lago, Imbabura

Tel: +593 6 291 8488

www.condenastjohansens.com/4volcanoes

COLOMBIA - BOLÍVAR (CARTAGENA DE INDIAS)

Hotel Boutique Bovedas de Santa Clara

Calle del Torno No. 39-29, Barrio San Diego, Cartagena de Indias, Bolívar

Tel: +57 5 650 44 65 Ext

www.condenastjohansens.com/bovedasdesantaclara

ECUADOR - PICHINCHA (QUITO)

Hotel Plaza Grande

Calle García Moreno, N5-16 y Chile, Pichincha, Quito

Tel: +593 2 2528 700

www.condenastjohansens.com/plazagrandequito

COLOMBIA - BOLÍVAR (CARTAGENA DE INDIAS)

Hotel LM

Centro Calle de la Mantilla No. 3-56, Cartagena de Indias, Bolívar

Tel: +57 5 664 9100/9564

www.condenastjohansens.com/hotellm

PERÚ - CUSCO (MACHU PICCHU PUEBLO)

Inkaterra Machu Picchu Pueblo Hotel

Machu Picchu Pueblo, Cusco

Tel: +51 1 610 0400

www.condenastjohansens.com/inkaterra

COLOMBIA - BOLÍVAR (CARTAGENA DE INDIAS)

Hotel San Pedro de Majagua

Isla Grande, Islas del Rosario, Cartagena de Indias, Bolívar

Tel: +57 5 650 44 65 Ext 4069-4009

www.condenastjohansens.com/hotelmajagua

PERÚ - LIMA (LIMA)

Swissôtel Lima

Via Central 150, Centro Empresarial Real, San Isidro, Lima 27

Tel: +511 421 4400

www.condenastjohansens.com/swissotellima

ECUADOR - BAHÍA DE CARÁQUEZ (MANABÍ)

Casa Ceibo Boutique Hotel & Spa

Km. 5, Ave. Sixto Durán Ballén, Manabí, Bahía de Caráquez

Tel: +593 5 2399 399

www.condenastjohansens.com/casaceibo

PERÚ - LIMA (VIÑAK)

Refugios Del Perú - Viñak Reichraming

Av. Emilio Cavenecia 225, Of. 321, San Isidro, Lima 27

Tel: +511 421 7777

www.condenastjohansens.com/refugiosdelperu

ECUADOR - GALÁPAGOS ISLANDS (SANTA CRUZ ISLAND)

Galápagos Safari Camp

Finca Palo Santo, Santa Cruz Island, Galápagos Islands

Tel: +593 9 371 7552

www.condenastjohansens.com/galapagossafaricamp

URUGUAY - MALDONADO (JOSÉ IGNACIO)

Casa Suaya

Ruta 10 Km 185, 5, José Ignacio

Tel: +598 4486 2750

www.condenastjohansens.com/casasuaya

Hotels - The Americas, Atlantic & Caribbean

Properties listed below can be found in our Recommended Hotels, Inns, Resorts & Spas – The Americas, Atlantic, Caribbean & Pacific 2012 Guide

URUGUAY - MALDONADO (PUNTA DEL ESTE)

L'Auberge

Carnoustie y Av. del Agua, Barrio Parque del Golf,
Punta del Este CP20100

Tel: +598 4248 8888

www.condenastjohansens.com/laubergeuruguay

CARIBBEAN - ANGUILLA (WEST END)

Sheriva Luxury Villas & Suites

Maundays Bay Road, West End AI-2640

Tel: +1 264 498 9898

www.condenastjohansens.com/sheriva

URUGUAY - MONTEVIDEO (MONTEVIDEO)

Don Boutique Hotel

Piedras 234, Montevideo, Montevideo

Tel: +598 2915 9999

www.condenastjohansens.com/donhotel

CARIBBEAN - ANTIGUA (ST. JOHN'S)

Blue Waters

P.O. Box 257, St. John's

Tel: +44 870 360 1245

www.condenastjohansens.com/bluewaters

VENEZUELA - PARQUE NACIONAL ARCHIPIÉLAGO LOS ROQUES
(LOS ROQUES)

Posada Acuarela

Calle Las Flores 87, Parque Nacional Archipiélago Los
Roques, Los Roques

Tel: +58 212 953 4235

www.condenastjohansens.com/posadaacuarela

CARIBBEAN - ANTIGUA (ST. JOHN'S)

Curtain Bluff

P.O. Box 288, St. John's

Tel: +1 268 462 8400

www.condenastjohansens.com/curtainbluff

ATLANTIC - BERMUDA (HAMILTON)

Rosedon Hotel

P.O. Box Hm 290, Hamilton Hmax

Tel: +1 441 295 1640

www.condenastjohansens.com/rosedonhotel

CARIBBEAN - ANTIGUA (ST. JOHN'S)

Galley Bay Resort & Spa

Five Islands, St. John's

Tel: +1 954 481 8787

www.condenastjohansens.com/galleybay

CARIBBEAN - ANGUILLA (LITTLE BAY)

Àni Villas

Little Bay

Tel: +1 264 497 7888

www.condenastjohansens.com/anivillas

CARIBBEAN - ANTIGUA (ST. JOHN'S)

The Inn at English Harbour

P.O. Box 187, St. John's

Tel: +1 268 460 1014

www.condenastjohansens.com/innatenglishharbour

CARIBBEAN - ANGUILLA (MAUNDAYS BAY)

Cap Juluca

Maundays Bay, AI-2640

Tel: +1 264 497 6666

www.condenastjohansens.com/capjuluca

CARIBBEAN - BARBADOS (CHRIST CHURCH)

Little Arches

Enterprise Beach Road, Christ Church

Tel: +1 246 420 4689

www.condenastjohansens.com/littlearches

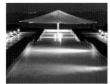

CARIBBEAN - ANGUILLA (RENDEZVOUS BAY)

CuisinArt Golf Resort & Spa

P.O. Box 2000, Rendezvous Bay

Tel: +1 264 498 2000

www.condenastjohansens.com/cuisinartresort

CARIBBEAN - BRITISH VIRGIN ISLANDS (PETER ISLAND)

Peter Island Resort and Spa

Peter Island

Tel: +616 458 6767

www.condenastjohansens.com/peterislandresort

CARIBBEAN - ANGUILLA (SANDY HILL BAY BEACH)

Bird of Paradise

Sandy Hill Bay Beach

Tel: +1 414 791 9461

www.condenastjohansens.com/birdofparadise

CARIBBEAN - BRITISH VIRGIN ISLANDS (PETER ISLAND)

The Villas at Peter Island

Peter Island

Tel: +616 458 6767

www.condenastjohansens.com/villaspeterisland

Hotels - Caribbean

Properties listed below can be found in our Recommended Hotels, Inns, Resorts & Spas – The Americas, Atlantic, Caribbean & Pacific 2012 Guide

CARIBBEAN - BRITISH VIRGIN ISLANDS (VIRGIN GORDA)

Biras Creek Resort

North Sound, Virgin Gorda

Tel: +1 248 364 2421

www.condenastjohansens.com/birascreek

CARIBBEAN - SAINT-BARTHÉLEMY (ANSE DE TOINY)

Hôtel Le Toiny

Anse de Toiny

Tel: +590 590 27 88 88

www.condenastjohansens.com/letoiny

CARIBBEAN - CAYMAN ISLANDS (GRAND CAYMAN)

Cotton Tree

375 Conch Point Road, P.O. Box 31324,
Grand Cayman KY1-1206

Tel: +1 345 943 0700

www.condenastjohansens.com/caymancottontree

CARIBBEAN - SAINT-BARTHÉLEMY (GRAND CUL DE SAC)

Hotel Guanahani & Spa

Grand Cul de Sac

Tel: +590 590 27 66 60

www.condenastjohansens.com/guanahani

CARIBBEAN - DOMINICAN REPUBLIC (PUERTO PLATA)

Casa Colonial Beach & Spa

P.O. Box 22, Puerto Plata

Tel: +1 809 320 3232

www.condenastjohansens.com/casacolonial

CARIBBEAN - SAINT-MARTIN (BAIE LONGUE)

La Samanna

P.O. Box 4077, 97064 CEDEX

Tel: +590 590 87 64 00

www.condenastjohansens.com/lasamanna

CARIBBEAN - GRENADA (ST. GEORGE'S)

Azzurra Castle

St. George's

Tel: +1 473 439 0000/9900

www.condenastjohansens.com/azzurracastle

CARIBBEAN - ST. LUCIA (CAP ESTATE)

Cap Maison Resort & Spa

Smugglers Cove Drive, Cap Estate, Gros Islet

Tel: +1 758 457 8670

www.condenastjohansens.com/capmaison

CARIBBEAN - GRENADA (ST. GEORGE'S)

LaSource

Pink Gin Beach, St. George's

Tel: +1 473 444 2556

www.condenastjohansens.com/lasource

CARIBBEAN - ST. LUCIA (SOUFRIÈRE)

Anse Chastanet

Soufrière

Tel: +1 758 459 7000/6100

www.condenastjohansens.com/ansechastanet

CARIBBEAN - GRENADA (ST. GEORGE'S)

Spice Island Beach Resort

Grand Anse Beach, St. George's

Tel: +1 473 444 4258/4423

www.condenastjohansens.com/spiceisland

CARIBBEAN - ST. LUCIA (SOUFRIÈRE)

The Hotel Chocolat

The Rabot Estate, P.O. Box 312, Soufrière

Tel: +44 844 544 1272

www.condenastjohansens.com/hotelchocolat

CARIBBEAN - JAMAICA (MONTEGO BAY)

The Tryall Club

P.O. Box 1206, Montego Bay

Tel: +1 876 956 5660

www.condenastjohansens.com/tryallclub

CARIBBEAN - ST. LUCIA (SOUFRIÈRE)

Jade Mountain at Anse Chastanet

Soufrière

Tel: +1 758 459 4000/6100

www.condenastjohansens.com/jademountain

CARIBBEAN - JAMAICA (OCHO RIOS)

Sandals Royal Plantation, Ocho Rios

Main Street , P.O. Box 2, Ocho Rios

Tel: +1 876 974 5601

www.condenastjohansens.com/sandalsroyalplantation

CARIBBEAN - ST. LUCIA (SOUFRIÈRE)

Ladera

Soufrière

Tel: +1 866 290 0978

www.condenastjohansens.com/ladera

Hotels - Caribbean & Pacific

Properties listed below can be found in our Recommended Hotels, Inns, Resorts & Spas – The Americas, Atlantic, Caribbean & Pacific 2012 Guide

CARIBBEAN - THE GRENADINES (BEQUIA)

Firefly Plantation

Bequia

Tel: +1 784 458 3414
www.condenastjohansens.com/fireflybequia

CARIBBEAN - THE GRENADINES (MUSTIQUE ISLAND)

Cotton House

Mustique Island

Tel: +1 784 456 4777
www.condenastjohansens.com/cottonhouse

CARIBBEAN - THE GRENADINES (MUSTIQUE ISLAND)

Firefly

Mustique Island

Tel: +1 784 488 8414
www.condenastjohansens.com/firefly

CARIBBEAN - THE GRENADINES (PALM ISLAND)

Palm Island

Palm Island

Tel: +1 954 481 8787
www.condenastjohansens.com/palmisland

CARIBBEAN - TURKS & CAICOS ISLANDS (GRACE BAY BEACH)

Gansevoort Turks + Caicos, a Wymara Resort

Lower Bight Road, Grace Bay Beach, Providenciales

Tel: +1 649 941 7555
www.condenastjohansens.com/gansevoorttc

CARIBBEAN - TURKS & CAICOS ISLANDS (GRACE BAY BEACH)

Grace Bay Club

Grace Bay Beach, P.O. Box 128, Providenciales

Tel: +1 649 946 5050
www.condenastjohansens.com/gracebayclub

CARIBBEAN - TURKS & CAICOS ISLANDS (GRACE BAY BEACH)

Point Grace

Grace Bay Beach, P.O. Box 700, Providenciales

Tel: +1 649 946 5096
www.condenastjohansens.com/pointgrace

CARIBBEAN - TURKS & CAICOS ISLANDS (GRACE BAY BEACH)

The Regent Palms, Turks & Caicos

Grace Bay Beach, P.O. Box 681, Providenciales

Tel: +649 946 8666
www.condenastjohansens.com/regentpalms

CARIBBEAN - TURKS & CAICOS ISLANDS (GRACE BAY BEACH)

The Somerset on Grace Bay

Grace Bay Beach, Princess Drive, Providenciales

Tel: +1 649 946 5900
www.condenastjohansens.com/somersetgracebay

CARIBBEAN - TURKS & CAICOS ISLANDS (PARROT CAY)

Parrot Cay & COMO Shambhala Retreat

P.O. Box 164, Providenciales

Tel: +1 649 946 7788
www.condenastjohansens.com/parrotcay

CARIBBEAN - TURKS & CAICOS ISLANDS (PROVIDENCIALES)

The West Bay Club

Lower Bight Road, Providenciales

Tel: +1 649 946 8550
www.condenastjohansens.com/thewestbayclub

CARIBBEAN - TURKS & CAICOS ISLANDS (WEST GRACE BAY BEACH)

Turks & Caicos Club

West Grace Bay Beach, P.O. Box 687, Providenciales

Tel: +1 649 946 5800
www.condenastjohansens.com/turksandcaicos

PACIFIC - FIJI ISLANDS (LABASA)

Nukubati Private Island Great Sea Reef

P.O. Box 1928, Labasa

Tel: +679 603 0919
www.condenastjohansens.com/nukubati

PACIFIC - FIJI ISLANDS (NADI)

The Fiji Orchid

Saweni Beach Road, Lautoka, Nadi

Tel: +679 664 0099
www.condenastjohansens.com/fijiorchid

PACIFIC - FIJI ISLANDS (QAMEA ISLAND)

Qamea Resort & Spa

P.A. Matei, Taveuni

Tel: +649 360 0858
www.condenastjohansens.com/qamea

PACIFIC - FIJI ISLANDS (YASAWA ISLANDS)

Turtle Island, Fiji

Turtle Island, Yasawa Islands

Tel: +1 360 256 4347
www.condenastjohansens.com/turtleisland

Hotels - Pacific

Properties listed below can be found in our Recommended Hotels, Inns, Resorts & Spas – The Americas, Atlantic, Caribbean & Pacific 2012 Guide

PACIFIC - VANUATU (EFATE ISLAND)

Eratap Beach Resort

Eratap Point, Port Vila, Efate Island

Tel: +678 554 5007

www.condenastjohansens.com/eratap

PACIFIC - VANUATU (EFATE ISLAND)

The Havannah Vanuatu

Samoa Point, P.O. Box 4, Port Vila, Efate Island

Tel: + 678 551 8060

www.condenastjohansens.com/thehavannah

Looking for the Perfect Gift...

Why not treat someone to our Gift Vouchers!

The perfect gift for birthdays, weddings and anniversaries for friends, family, special clients and colleagues.

Gift Vouchers are valid for one year and are redeemable against most hotel services within our portfolio of Recommended Hotels, Spas, Villas & Venues including accommodation and dining.

Vouchers are available in denominations of £100, £50, €140, €70, $150, $75 and may be used as payment or part payment for your stay or a meal at any Condé Nast Johansens 2012 recommended property.

Spend over £200 and receive a complimentary hotel guide of your choice.

For more information visit
www.condenastjohansens.com/gift-vouchers

Other Condé Nast Johansens Guides

To purchase Guides please call +44 (0)208 955 7067
or visit our Bookshop at www.condenastjohansens.com/books

A British love affair

We all have a love affair with sleep, yet many of us never truly experience a deep uninterrupted night's sleep, night after night. At Hypnos each Royally Approved bed is individually handmade by master craftsmen using the finest natural materials to guarantee years of sumptuous and rejuvenating slumber. So, to be sure that you have the very best night's sleep, and awake feeling revitalised and refreshed, visit your local Hypnos Retailer and choose a Hypnos bed that's just right for you. Hypnos – the God of Sleep.

Hypnos is proud to be Condé Nast Johansens
Preferred Partner for beds and mattresses.

BY APPOINTMENT TO
HER MAJESTY
QUEEN ELIZABETH II
BEDDING AND UPHOLSTERY
MANUFACTURERS

HYPNOS®

THE MOST COMFORTABLE BEDS IN THE WORLD

www.hypnosbeds.com

Index by Property

Index by Property

Index by Location

England

Index by Location

Index by Location